PRACTICE SALES OF TEXAS

I hope you enjoy this book as the valuable tool it is intended to be.

My name is **Mac Winston** and I am **President of Practice Sales of Texas, LLC**, a dental practice valuation, transition and placement services firm based in Texas. I produced, edited and served as the primary contributing author for this book in 2009 with contributions from knowledgeable professionals around the US. These professionals have between them over 300 years of service in support of the dental community (information on these various contributors are detailed in pages 197 through 210).

During the last 20 years I have facilitated the purchase and sale of over 1,000 general and specialty dental practices throughout the US, and have even owned and subsequently sold two dental practices. In 2012 I formed Practice Sales of Texas to assist dentists in my home state in the sale, purchase and valuation of dental practices, as well as in employment placement.

I am pleased to say that the majority of my dental clients would describe me as a trusted confidant, consultant and virtual partner as they worked their way through practice acquisitions and the often difficult day to day challenges of operating their practices.

If I may be of assistance to you and your practice please contact me at:

9303 New Trails Drive, Suite 375, The Woodlands, TX 77381
Phone (866) 756-7412   Fax (281) 466-1946
practicesalesoftexas.com

TO: Baylor Class of 2013   October 18, 2012

"The
AFFLUENT
Dentist s"

Your guide to building, growing, transitioning and reaping
the benefits of a healthy, wealthy dental practice

From: Jennifer Loyall
Jennifer @ TDAmemberinsure.com

Produced and Edited by PPC LOAN
Authored by PPC LOAN and Members of ADS
With Contributions From Various Others

Published by PPC LOAN

9303 New Trails Drive, Suite 375
The Woodlands, TX 77381

Cover design by BrandExtract, LLC
Book design by BrandExtract, LLC

ISBN: 978-0-615-33680-0

First Edition

Printed in the United States of America

Contents

Chapter 4

Chapter 5

Chapter 6

Chapter 7

Chapter 8

Chapter 9

Chapter 10

Creating and Realizing Practice Value Through Practice Management   145

Chapter 11

Chapter 12

Chapter 13

The
AFFLUENT
Dentist

CHAPTER 1

Changes, Challenges and Tremendous Opportunity

Few professions can equal the financial and emotional rewards a career in dentistry presently offers. Never in the history of dentistry has there been so much opportunity! In short, it's a great time to be a dentist.

Dentistry is at its peak in terms of:

- *Earnings Power*
  Dentistry has surpassed many professions, including medicine and law, in terms of personal annual income. Some dentists earn $500,000 to $1 million, and a few earn even more. Moreover, the hourly earnings potential of a dentist is virtually unsurpassed. Even when one considers the technical expertise and non-clinical aspects required to operate a practice, the rate of compensation per hour is exceptional! This is particularly true for practitioners who wish to work on a part-time basis. Dentistry allows dentists the ability to work part-time, earn a great income, pursue other outside interests, and realize options in retirement not available to other less portable careers.

- *Practice Value*

Not only can a dentist earn a handsome income from ownership, he or she also can build a business that is constantly increasing in value. Even though the average practice values as a percentage of gross income have declined in recent years, the absolute value of dental practices has increased substantially. For example, a practice producing $150,000 per year in 1970 may have sold for 75% of production. Today, the average practice may sell for a lower percentage of gross (68%), yet the practice's annual production typically exceeds $500,000 to $600,000. Thus, in real dollars, the practice has a greater value today than ever before.

- *Demand for Dental Services*

Despite the ups and downs of the U.S. economy, the demand for dentists and dental services continues to grow just as most regions of the country are beginning to experience a shortage of dentists. Three key factors fueling the increasing demand for dental services are the steady growth in the population of the U.S., aging Baby Boomers (now in their 50s and 60s), and a growing population of educated consumers desiring quality dental care and willing to pay for these services.

A Major Demographic Shift Is Under Way

Due to government promoted increased enrollment in dental schools, thousands of dentists graduated in the 1960s and 1970s resulting in a glut in the 1970s, 1980s and early 1990s. The increased numbers of dentists in the population contributed to a highly competitive market in which advertising was introduced, discount dentistry was offered, clinics and dental office chains were opened, insurance companies entered the dental marketplace, and Wall Street consolidators tried to skim the profits from the dental profession.

Baby boomer dentists who graduated in the '60s, '70s, and '80s are now reaching retirement age. Statistics show that until the middle of this decade, the number of new dental school graduates has been exceeding the number of those retiring each year. However, the number of dental retirees for 2007 and beyond will begin to exceed the number of dental graduates as the baby boomer enrollment bulge of the 20th century is mirrored in a retirement bulge early in the 21st century.

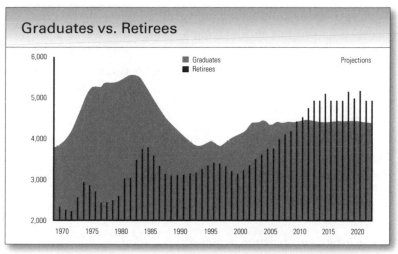

Graph from "The Future of Dentistry," By Eric S. Solomon, DDS, MA, in *Dental Economics,* November 2004

The Good News

For the three following reasons this "new versus retiring dentists" scenario is one of the best things to ever happen to dentists:

1. The demand for dental services continues to steadily increase in step with increases in U.S. population and the increase in the dental IQ of American consumers. Concurrently, there is a decrease in the number of dental care providers. These two factors are greatly increasing the demand for dental care per provider. This increased demand means that for the first time in many years, dentists are able to charge what they deserve for their services.

2. There are more dental practices on the market, giving new dentists a greater range of acquisition opportunities.

3. In many parts of the country, the increased demand for dental services has made practice startups economically competitive with the purchasing of an existing practice.

Implications for Sales of Dental Practices

With retirees outnumbering new graduates, the market for U.S. dental practices has shifted from a "seller's market" to a "buyer's market," with some markets such as southern California bucking the trend from time to time. The net effect of this shift is a slowing in the speed with which practices are sold, and a reduction in the value for which a practice can be sold relative to its gross receipts.

As with the typical consumer, dentists today are shopping for the best practice at the least cost possible. Therefore, unless an existing dental practice is an "optimum practice," it may be more difficult to sell in a timely manner and/or for a price acceptable to the selling dentist. An optimum practice can be defined as one that:

- is located in an urban or suburban market,
- is well-managed,
- has state-of-the-art equipment,
- has gross receipts of $650,000 or more (with no reduced fee plans), and
- has operating expenses (not including wages for dentists, expenses unrelated to the production of dental receipts, or payments of interest expense on practice debt) equal to 65% or less of total receipts.

Implications for Rural America

The impact of the demographic shift occurring in dentistry is felt hardest in rural America, where many dentists are retiring without replacements.

The majority of prospective buyers for dental practices were born, reared and educated in urban and suburban markets and thus do not perceive the merits of practicing dentistry and raising a family in a rural area. This is leaving many rural areas underserviced even though rural markets typically offer the following benefits:

- Reduced competition for patients
- Lower cost of living
- Lower employee costs
- Lower office rent expense
- Strong patient loyalty
- Strong collection percentages
- Quality lifestyle

To illustrate the advantages of practicing in rural America, take the case of a dentist who first settled in St. George, Utah, a rapidly growing retirement area. He was competing with dozens of other dentists for the same patients and was unable to grow his practice to the level he wanted. He heard about an opportunity in rural Kansas, where he had grown up. He relocated and within months was busier and making more money than he had dreamed possible.

Some dentists have suggested that rural America won't accept the same type of dentistry that they want to practice, but this is not the case. In fact, it appears that trust in the "country dentist" is so great that if he or she says a procedure needs to be done, the patient feels it must be so.

As a person decides where to live, he or she should decide what is truly important to them, how they want to live, and where and how they want to raise a family. In other words, they need to determine "what really matters in life." Country living can provide a dentist with the opportunity to have a very successful practice and to enjoy a superior quality of life. In fact, rural America represents an excellent opportunity for those new graduates just getting their careers under way or for mature dentists looking for a new pace of life or practice activity (see the "Green Acres Retirement Strategy" in Chapter 10).

Implications for Smaller Practices

In the latter part of the 1980s and early 1990s, many new dentists in the market to purchase a dental practice were looking for a practice grossing $75,000 to $200,000 per year that they could gradually build up to a satisfactory level of productivity. Therefore, practices in this range of receipts were quickly purchased as they came to market. This trend has changed, as today's young dentists wish to generate strong personal incomes from the start. Therefore, solo practices with gross annual receipts of $450,000 to $750,000 and net incomes of 40% or more are in greater demand than those with lesser receipts and net income.

Practice Sales and the Portable Nature of the Dental Trade

In the past, it was customary for most dentists to start or purchase a practice, stay in the same area, and sell the practice 25 to 40 years later. Therefore, virtually all dental practice sales occurred as a result of the death or retirement of the seller.

Today, an increasing number of dentists, ranging in age from 35 to 55, are selling their practices well in advance of retirement in order to accommodate family, lifestyle and/or professional needs (to pursue a change in climate or size of community, move closer to family, change in sophistication of patients, change in lifestyle, etc.). In other words, more and more dentists today have identified and are utilizing the value inherent in the portability of their trade skill. They are willing to make changes that few of their predecessors made in the past. Here are some examples:

- A successful, 47-year-old dentist in the mid-Atlantic area practiced in the third largest metropolitan area in the United States. For several years, the dentist and his spouse had vacationed in Oregon and Washington states. Their children had recently finished college, and one had moved to the West Coast. The dentist and his wife wanted a change in lifestyle and a break from the dense traffic. Within six months, this dentist was able to sell his practice and his home above the appraised values because of the demand for both dental practices and real estate in the area and moved to the West Coast.

• A 34-year-old practitioner and his spouse decided to sell their practice, which grossed $900,000 a year in a small rural community in the Northeast. They wanted to live in a metropolitan area with a moderate climate. They wished to make the move before their children reached school age. This dentist sold his practice to an associate and continued to work in the practice while he and his wife searched for a new practice. They also sold their home and rented so they could be free to act when an opportunity presented itself. Due to the untimely death of a dentist in the metropolitan area of their choice, they found a practice to suit their needs. They purchased the practice and a new home, and began anew.

• A 40-year-old dentist practiced in the Midwest for 14 years and vacationed in warm climates each year. This dentist and his spouse decided to move to a warmer climate and an area that would better support his focus on cosmetic dentistry. A professional transition consultant valued the dentist's Midwest practice and found a buyer. After an extensive demographic study by the transition consultant located the desired climate and market, this dentist and his wife relocated and started a practice.

These are just three examples of hundreds of practice sales occurring where the motivation of the seller is to relocate and continue practicing dentistry. Other dentists have sold their practices to start a new profession in teaching, financial services, consulting, real estate sales or accounting.

The Bottom Line

It's a great time to be a dentist! A dental degree leads to many career options, and opportunities are plentiful for practitioners at any stage of their career. As the demand for dentistry is steadily growing and the public becomes increasingly enamored with a "pretty smile," dentists are earning higher incomes, and their practices are selling for higher prices.

CHAPTER 2

Owning Your Own Practice

Dentists today have a wide range of choices in their careers. Most new dental school graduates who immediately go into practice will become associates in order to hone their dental care delivery skills and to learn the business of dentistry before purchasing or opening their own offices. Some will join the military or go to work as employees for schools, corporations or the government. Others will join a group practice as partners or take the plunge into owning their own solo practices, either by starting one from scratch or purchasing all or a portion of an existing practice.

No matter which of these paths a dentist takes immediately out of dental school, at some point most dentists will take the plunge into practice ownership. When and what option of practice ownership is selected depends on the dentist's personal situation (the circumstances, goals, dreams and other factors that are unique to that individual).

There are tremendous opportunities offered by owning your own practice with numerous rewards. However, the pursuit of ownership should be conducted in a purposeful manner. An informed and thorough approach will lead to success and financial stability, while a misinformed or hasty approach can cause financial distress and a career fraught with unnecessary emotional stress and struggles.

Becoming an Associate

Advantages	Disadvantages
• No investment required	• Cannot always do things your own way
• Opportunity to build speed and skills	• Income is usually limited
• Opportunity to learn from another's successes and failures	• May be limited in services that can be performed
• Holding pattern for the right opportunity	• No tax benefits
• Usually does not require binding commitment	• Usually restricted by covenant not to compete

A Few Words of Caution

Owning a practice is a powerful dream, and one that easily can become a reality, but a few words of caution are in order. First, dentists should beware the allure of the sense of autonomy inherent in this dream. As any dentist who has borrowed money to become an owner of a practice will report, there is no such thing as absolute independence. Second, the dream of ownership quickly can turn into the nightmares of bankruptcy, overdrawn bank accounts, disrupted family life and depression when dentists decide to purchase or start a practice before they are ready.

While it is generally understood that there is less risk in buying an existing practice than in starting one from scratch, every year there are practice acquisition transactions that fail. Therefore, dentists should thoroughly understand the challenges involved before making a choice to become a dental practice owner. Working as an associate for two or three years following graduation can be a very valuable investment of time and effort in terms of sharpening skills and gaining firsthand knowledge of the challenges, benefits and drawbacks to ownership.

Advantages of Practice Ownership

Owning all or part of a practice is attractive for many reasons, including:

- *Custom Fit*
A dentist can adopt the type of facility, business and clinical philosophy, and schedule most desired.

- *Personal Income*
Most practice owners have a greater net income than dentists who work for someone else. Practice owners should make between 50% and 60% on their own personal production. Thus, all things being equal, owners can earn up to two to three times more than associate dentists.

- *Personal Wealth*
Dentists who own their own practices are building personal wealth through both the increasing market value of the practice and the substantial personal income generated from the practice. Non-owner dentists have no opportunity to benefit from practice value, and as noted, their personal income is generally less than that of owners.

- *Favorable Tax Environment*
When you own a practice, many expenses are tax deductible or depreciable that do not apply for dental associate employees. These deductions include pension plans, dues, insurance, continuing education, car leases, travel, entertainment and meals.

- *Ease of Entry*
Financing the purchase of a practice is easy. Some dentists make the mistake of looking at their small to non-existent net worth, high level of personal debt (predominantly student loans) and hefty monthly expenses, and are reluctant to pursue ownership because they believe financing is unavailable. Not so. There are

a few financial institutions that understand the dental industry and why buyers have little or no net worth; most importantly, they recognize that the match of a dental practice with the skills of a capable dentist represents a sound lending opportunity. As a result, practice acquisition loans are readily available at very competitive interest rates.

• *Control*
You have control over what happens in your own practice.

• *Pride of Ownership*
A less tangible reason to own a practice is pride of ownership. Anyone who owns a home understands why people take greater care and pride in things that they own rather than those that they rent or lease. Planning, designing and growing a dental practice can give you a great sense of pride and accomplishment.

Start from Scratch or Buy an Existing Practice?

Let's say you are at the point where you are ready to own a practice. Buying or starting your practice is likely to be one of the most critical business and financial moves you will ever make. It is important to remember that having exemplary clinical skills does not guarantee success as a dental practice owner. A dentist must also focus on business operations and be prepared to make good management decisions.

What are the merits of starting a practice as opposed to purchasing an existing one? A careful look at the following examples will help answer this question.

A Comparative Example
• *Dr. A decides to start a practice in a popular growing community.*
An attractive space is available, and demographics indicate a need for an additional dentist. Dr. A leases 1,500 square feet to accommodate future expansion. He qualifies for a $340,000 loan to fund the leasehold improvements, working capital, equipment,

supplies and furniture. The monthly debt service on this loan is approximately $4,353 (based on a 10-year term with a fixed note rate of 9.25%). Dr. A begins operations with minimal staff. He promotes the practice in several ways and has the personal and technical skills necessary to attract patients. Within three months, the practice has the astounding new patient flow of 35 patients per month. He is pleased and feels confident that the practice will be successful.

• *Dr. B chooses to purchase an existing practice.*
The practice has a competent staff and historical receipts that total $600,000 a year. The practice has four days of hygiene production per week, with approximately 1,200 active patients (defined as patients seen at least once during the last 18 months). The new patient flow is 15 to 20 patients per month or 210 per year. The practice has four operatories and most of the equipment is 12 years old. The annual profit margin (profit before compensation for professional dental services rendered) is 40% or $240,000. The agreed-upon price for the practice is $430,000, with an additional $60,000 to be paid for the practice's accounts receivable. Dr. B is approved for a $510,000 loan to cover 100% of the purchase price of both the practice and receivables plus various practice acquisition transaction costs of $20,000. The monthly payment will be approximately $6,323 (based on a 10-year term with a fixed note rate of 8.5%).

On the surface, it may appear that Dr. A's new practice is the better choice. Dr. A has the benefit of new improvements and equipment, great new patient flow, and smaller monthly debt payments. However, a closer look reveals a somewhat different story.

First, let's look at patient flow. Experienced consultants usually agree that the patient attrition rate of an established practice, or a practice in transition to new ownership, runs between 7% and 10%. However, the attrition rate for patients in a new practice is in the range of 15% to 20% due to the greater concentration of immature/new patient relationships. Therefore, the core growth rate (growth adjusted for attrition) for Dr. A's practice will be roughly 30 patients per month (at an attrition rate of 15%), for a first-year total of 360. Meanwhile, Dr. B's attrition rate is 10% or 120 of the original active patient base of 1,200; however, this is offset by the historical new patient flow of 210 per year. Dr. B, therefore, will have an active patient total of roughly 1,250 at the end of his first year in the practice. Assuming the extraordinary pace of 35 new patients per month is maintained, it will still take Dr. A three to four years to reach the active patient total that Dr. B will realize just one year following the completion of his acquisition transaction. Furthermore, since the billings for work typically performed on new patients in no way equals what is initially spent in time and money to get them in the door, a heavy flow of new patients represents quite a challenge for a dental practice's front desk staff. New patients have questions to ask of the staff and vice versa, there is paperwork that must be completed, and an insurance form and health history work-up must be completed. Startup practices need to anticipate this challenge, as most patients seen will be new patients.

Starting a Practice

Advantages	Disadvantages
• Can be built very near to your choice of location	• No (or negative) cash flow to start
• Can be designed to your exact specs (office layout, equipment, décor, etc.)	• Need to hire and train staff
	• Negative equity position initially – you owe more than the value of the practice
• Ability to build your own team	• Incur leasehold improvement costs that accrue to landlord
	• More difficult to finance, and greater working capital requirements

Now let's look at income. We'll assume that Dr. A outperformed the expected or customary performance of a new practice, generating an impressive $300,000 in receipts in his first year of operations. His net income before compensation for dental services rendered is equally impressive at 45% of receipts, or $135,000, largely because he has no hygiene salary expense. Dr. A's total principal and interest payments for the first year are $52,236; thus, the net income/cash flow from the practice available to cover Dr. A's personal income needs is a solid $82,764. Meanwhile, Dr. B continues to operate the purchased practice as it had been functioning under the previous owner. Its annual receipts remain at $600,000 and its income before compensation for professional dental services remain at 40% of receipts. This leaves Dr. B with $240,000 to cover business debt payments and his personal living expenses. After providing for the annual debt service of $75,876, Dr. B is left with a personal income of $164,124.

Purchasing an Existing Practice

Pros	Cons
• Shorter decision tree	• Limited availability within desired dental care delivery market and time frame
• Instant patient base	
• Instant stream of business	
• Instant stream of cash flow	• Purchasing the seller's business and clinical reputation ("for better or worse")
• Instant experienced staff	
• Management/marketing support from seller (transition period following sale, seller letter, etc.)	
	• Possible ill-fitted or outdated equipment
• Proven market potential and site effectiveness	• The challenge of fitting into a preexisting dental office staff family, unaware of the family dynamics
• Ongoing business momentum	
	• Entering cold into a rapid day-to-day business and clinical operating pace

Another Example

A senior dental student had several instructors encourage him to start a practice upon graduation. Later, he was well along in the process when he heard there was an excellent practice for sale nearby. He was intrigued and tempted by this acquisition opportunity, but felt it was too late to turn back. He had already located a vacant space for the startup in a shopping center in a nice part of town, was working with a dental supply house to design the space to his satisfaction, and had other plans in the works.

By the time this new dentist opens his startup practice, he will have:

- completed improvements to the space, providing for three plumbed operatory spaces (two fully equipped and one available for future growth),
- purchased all new office furnishings, a computer and attendant software,
- hired staff (An experienced receptionist to run the front desk, including making appointments and completing the insurance, is critical. Some startups include a chairside assistant from the beginning while others wait until the pace of care has picked up sufficiently to justify the hire. The addition of a hygienist is definitely a hire to be made well after the startup is operating at a healthy pace), and
- purchased all new dental equipment and required supplies.

All of this, including funds necessary to cover operating expenses and the dentist s personal income needs, has been financed with a loan totaling $325,000. In addition to the startup practice debt, the young dentist still has roughly $125,000 in outstanding student loans. Clearly, it is important that the practice expand quickly for the young dentist to survive. The longer it takes to turn a profit, the more pressure the young dentist will feel.

Initially, other than family and friends, the young dentist will have few patients. By implementing advertising and becoming involved in the community, he will begin to attract new patients. As the practice grows, he will add staff and eventually will be able to afford a part-time hygienist.

As is the case with this young dentist, every startup begins with a great deal of uncertainty regarding new patients, collections and cash flow — and yet success is almost wholly dependent upon a positive outcome in these three areas. With the growth of suburban America, opportunities clearly exist to initiate successful practice startups, and many dentists are taking advantage of these opportunities. However, in areas where there are reasonable opportunities to purchase existing dental practices, the argument is strongly in favor of acquiring a practice as the level of uncertainty regarding future patient flow, collections and cash flow is greatly diminished by comparison.

Practice Acquisition

Most dentists interested in buying a dental practice gravitate toward heavily populated urban areas and closely linked suburban markets. Examples are the metropolitan areas of Chicago, Dallas, Atlanta, Denver, Phoenix, Los Angeles and St. Louis. Young dentists like to be close to high school and college friends, family, major entertainment and shopping centers, the dental school, and other areas that meet their personal and social ideals. However, the financial and clinical fulfillment of a dentist's potential will always be optimized where there are plenty of patients in need of dental care and ready to pay for it.

There are huge numbers of people in need of quality dental care in rural markets, but rural markets are chosen less frequently by prospective practice buyers because they are "out there" where there might be few of the most desirable lifestyle characteristics of metropolitan areas. Many rural practices do, however, offer a significant investment opportunity not available in most urban and suburban practices.

The cash flow of a dental practice generally improves (e.g., more money is made doing the same work), and the market value of a practice (sales price) generally declines the farther away its location is from an urban center. Cash flow improves largely because of reductions in rent and staff expense. Market value declines because there are fewer buyers for rural practices. This gap between a dental practice's economic value (the practice's value as a generator of cash flow into the future) and its market value represents the investment opportunity that often is not available in the urban and suburban practice. Dentists in rural markets often realize a larger disposable income, a larger personal savings rate, and an earlier retirement than their counterparts in urban and suburban practices.

Focus Your Search

As soon as you've decided to become a practice buyer, it's a good idea to get in touch with a practice broker active in the markets that are most attractive to you. (See Chapter 3 for more information on how a broker can assist you.) In addition, answering the following questions will help you narrow down the most desirable attributes of a practice:

- How many operatories do I want?
- What do I want the flow of the office to look like?
- What kind of image do I want to project?
- Is the décor important?
- Does it matter if it is a leased space or a building?
- What systems are important to me?
- Can I practice without a computer for a short period of time?
- Do I understand the components of overhead?
- What are my financial needs for income?
- Will the practice net support my income needs and the debt service?
- Will I be hiring my own representation (broker, accountant or attorney)?

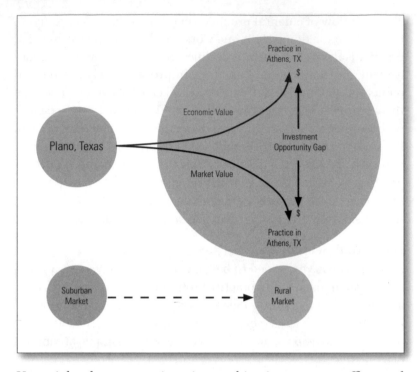

You might also want to imagine working in your own office, and ask such questions as:

- What does the office look like?
- How does it feel?
- How many employees are there?
- What does the equipment look like?

With the answer to these and other questions, you should create a report card of the items that are important to you and grade them on a scale of 1 to 5, with 5 the lowest and 1 the highest degree of priority. It's important that the grading be realistic and grounded in what is truly most important to you.

The Hunt

With this scoring system in place and a practice broker identified, you are ready to visit practices and prioritize observations of each. Before considering even one practice, however, you need to accept that there is no perfect practice. Buyers should not set out on a quest for their "dream practice," but rather a practice that serves basic needs and has the potential to fulfill their dream. To do otherwise is to risk never being satisfied in the search.

Buyers who stay focused on those key attributes will simplify the search and find a desired practice more quickly. For instance, a practice's market, clinical focus and office square footage are much more difficult (and in some cases impossible) to change, whereas old equipment can always be updated or replaced, office space spruced up, computer equipment added and spare operatories fitted out. Likewise, the physical layout of the practice is more important than the appearance, which, like the equipment, can be changed with reasonable expense to suit the owner's desires.

The Fit

Individual dentists have greatly increased their productivity over the last decade, thanks to increasingly sophisticated technology and expanded duty staff. Adding annual increases in billing rates to this, it's no wonder that a large number of single-dentist practices now generate over $1 million in collections and that an even larger number generate over $675,000.

As these large practices are put on the market for sale, the two biggest questions on prospective buyers' minds are:

- Can I produce what the seller is producing?
- Can I afford this practice?

An answer of YES to BOTH questions is NECESSARY in order for a practice to change hands.

To address these questions, a buyer needs to dissect the seller's current production and collections and evaluate his or her relative capacity and level of skill, as well as investigate the practice's cash flow as it relates to his or her own personal income needs and the price being asked for the practice. Consider the following example:

A general dentistry practice is being offered for sale at a price of $675,000, or 75% of its $900,000 annual gross collections. The practice's hygienist generates 20% of collections or $180,000 per annum, and the remainder is generated by the sole owner/operator general dentist (the equivalent of roughly $66,000 in monthly production). The typical buyer will secure 100% financing for the purchase price plus an additional $100,000 for working capital and transactional costs (since the typical buyer does not purchase the historical accounts receivable of the seller).

12 Months		
Hygiene	$ 180,000	20%
Dental	$ 720,000	80%
Total Collections	**$ 900,000**	100%

Practice Purchase Price	$ 675,000
Working Capital and Closing Cost Requirements	$ 100,000
Total Practice Acquisition Loan	$ 775,000
Annual Loan Payment Requirements	$ (146,113)

Can I Produce What the Seller Is Producing?
Assuming the buyer for this practice plans to work five days a week and 48 weeks a year, the total dentist work days per annum would be 240. Dividing the seller's $720,000 in annual collections for dental services rendered by 240 days equals daily collections of $3,000. Dividing this daily collections result by the practice's collections on production rate of 95% reveals a daily production rate of $3,158. This figure alone can be very helpful to buyers as they compare their daily production experience with that required by the practice in question.

Doctor Collections	$ 720,000
Doctor Work Days	240
Doctor Daily Collections	$ 3,000
Collections on Production	95%
Doctor Daily Production	$ 3,158

Doctor Daily Production	$ 3,158
Average Annual Production per Patient	$ 375
Patients Seen by the Dentist Each Day	8.4

Yet another figure can be derived that will greatly assist buyers in the evaluation of the practice's historical production relative to their own capabilities and interests. The average production per patient per annum for the typical general dentistry practice is $375. By dividing this figure into the daily production rate for the practice it can be generally determined that the dentist is seeing an average of 8.4 patients per day.

This last exercise in evaluating the seller production can be very revealing. Take for example a not uncommon situation where the buyer has divided the seller's production by $375 and determined that the seller must be seeing 20 patients per day, but the seller only reports seeing an average of 12. What typically ends up solving this mystery is the discovery that, although the seller has reported the production of an even mix of usual and customary dental services, he has in fact generated a great deal more crown and bridge revenue relative to that generated from all other work than he realized. The prospective buyer can then increase the production per patient figure to $650 for instance, and the resulting daily patient count is reduced to a more realistic figure. Without breaking down the seller's daily production to per-patient units, this realization would have never been made and thus a critical bit of information in the buyer's determination of his or her fit with the practice would have gone unnoticed. Had the sale occurred, and the buyer not had the persuasive or speed of crown and bridge delivery abilities of the seller, a significant shrinkage of daily production would have occurred.

Can I Afford This Practice?

After closing on the acquisition of a general dentistry practice, the new owner will need, first and foremost, to do three things to stay afloat:

- Pay the practice expenses necessary in the production of dental revenues (rent, lab, dental supplies, staff wages, etc.)
- Pay the monthly principal and interest due on the practice acquisition loan
- Pay himself or herself a wage sufficient to meet the base living expense needs

To do this consistently each month there must be sufficient cash flow to meet these costs plus provide some cushion for the inevitable fluctuations in monthly collections and expenses.

While the practice being considered generates total collections per annum of $900,000, it also generates expenses, not including the compensation of the owner/producer dentists, equal to 60% of collections or $540,000. (The typical general dentistry practice will experience an overhead rate of between 60% and 65% of collections.) This leaves $360,000 to meet the annual living expense needs of the new owner and his or her annual payment requirement on the practice acquisition loan. Subtracting the $146,113 in annual principal and interest paid on the practice acquisition loan leaves $213,887 for the new owner to cover personal living expense needs. Ideally, these living expense needs will not exceed $180,000 as a cushion of cash flow is necessary to ensure smooth bill paying each month.

Collections	$ 900,000
Overhead Expense	$ (540,000)
Net Discretionary Cash Flow (DCF)	**$ 360,000**
Practice Acquisition Debt Service	$ (146,000)
Owner's Wage Need	$ (180,000)
Net DCF after Owner's Comp and Debt Service	**$ 34,000**

A prospective buyer has any number of factors to consider when evaluating a dental practice, but let us emphasize again that two clear hurdles must be cleared before any other factors are relevant. The first is that the monthly production, number of patients seen per day, and mix of care delivered by the seller must correlate with the experience and expertise of the prospective buyer. The second is that the buyer's annual personal income needs must be a fit with the funds available for that purpose. Again, the answers to both "Can I produce what the seller is producing?" and "Can I afford this practice?" must be "yes" before a buyer can even think of closing on a practice acquisition transaction.

A New Tool for Determining Clinical Fit

The clinical fit of buyers with their desired practices is and will always be one of the most important factors to be considered in transitions of ownership. In fact, most difficulties experienced by new owners following a practice sale involve, to some degree, their struggle to get up to pace with the prior owners' speed of care delivery, unique clinical flair or expertise, etc. A new due diligence tool called PracticeBooster® offered by Dr. Charles Blair (visit Practice Booster.com) measures the area of Clinical Treatment Intensity of a practice. The Clinical Treatment Intensity of a practice is simply how the dentistry is done in a given practice. In effect, the PracticeBooster® uses the Clinical Treatment Intensifier^{SM} (CTI^{SM}) technology to measure the unique clinical treatment tendencies of the dentist/hygienist and compares them by percentile to their peers. No one has measured clinical treatment before (except dental insurance companies) with their "profiling" and "watch lists." The unique Percentile Ranker^{SM} provides percentile feedback for each of the Monitors, based on participating practices and Dr. Blair's 3,500 practice database (sampled). For instance, a 60th percentile match indicates they exceed 60% of dentists for that particular clinical parameter. With this new information, the prospective buyer or seller can obtain an accurate reading of where the practice is clinically, prior to purchasing or selling.

Digging into the Details with a Practice Audit

Every practice has both positive and negative characteristics, and the practice audit represents the opportunity for you to dig beneath the surface and discover additional facts about the practice and/or to verify claims.

Here are the ground rules when it comes to auditing a practice for potential purchase:

- *The Buyer Should Expect Complete Disclosure*

This means that you and your representatives in the process should have complete access to the practice, including access to the computer system, charts, staff interviews and tax returns.

- *The Buyer Must be Well Prepared for the Audit*

This means that you must know in advance what questions you need to have answered and develop a plan for getting those answers, as going back to the seller or the practice multiple times

Information that Buyers Need

- 3 years' historical tax returns for the practice and most recent interim operating statement for the year of sale (at a minimum)
- Copy of practice's most recent accounts receivable aging report
- Listing of furniture and equipment to be sold and their appraised value
- Details regarding staff, including names, salaries, benefits, years with the practice, etc.
- Listing of all DMO and standard indemnity insurance plans that practice is involved with
- Open access to all dental patient records of the practice
- Reason the seller is selling the practice
- The opportunity to walk through the practice and re-review all patient records and the appointment book immediately prior to the sale
- Copy of the draft letter of introduction and recommendation from the seller to the patient base of the practice regarding the buyer

to check on something not covered the first time around is not something sellers want to put up with or, in many cases, will allow.

• *All the Information Should be Evaluated in Terms of How Well the Practice Will Support the Buyer's Goals and Vision*
You should not be swayed by visions of great cash flow if the practice will not support your vision of how and where you want to practice dentistry.

Once the ground rules are covered, take these four steps to audit a dental practice targeted for acquisition:

• *First, Examine the Practice's Financial Reports*
This should include an interim income statement (a statement of collections and all practice expenses) reflecting total collections and practice expenses from January 1 to the end of a month and no further back than three months from the date that you begin your review of the practice (so if you are looking at the financials of a practice in September, you will want to receive an interim income statement from the seller reflecting total collections and expense for the practice for the six months that ended June 30 of that same year). In a few instances, the seller will not have systems in place to produce an income statement during the course of the year. If this occurs, you should request a monthly production and collections report for the practice through the month prior to the month you begin your review.

Additional financial reports that should be secured and reviewed include the last three years' tax returns for the practice (only the Schedule C section of the seller's personal tax return is required for practices being operated as sole proprietorships) and any related or supporting notes/schedules, and the accounts receivable aging report. Given the specialized nature of the work involved in evaluating these financial reports, most buyers are best served by providing this information to their practice acquisition consultants and/or accountants to review and report their findings.

- *Second, Examine the Practice's Patient Files*

Who would want to buy a practice without knowing the number of active patients? The major portion of the price paid for a dental practice is attributed to patient records, since patients and the cash flow generated from treating them are the reason an existing practice has value.

Most dentists do not really know how many active patient files they have. However, a good practice broker or practice consultant can assist a buyer in determining how to compile valuable patient information. A step-by-step procedure for gathering accurate information from a specific practice can be created. For example, the parameters for an "active patient" can be carefully defined. A sample of the files can be examined. In addition, a good practice consultant can assist in securing a contract agreement stating that if the selling dentist significantly misrepresents the information in the summary report, he or she may be liable for damages to the buyer.

You and, if you have one, your practice acquisition consultant should focus on the following when auditing a practice's patient files: treatment type, date of last visit, and appointment patterns noted in patient charts, X-rays, the insurance payors, a treatment plan compliance rate (85% or better is desired), and the active patient total for the practice.

The active patient total is typically determined by taking a cross section of all patient files and counting the number seen within the last 12, 18 or 24 months. Verification of the active patient total observed through the audit and claimed by the seller is done by dividing the total collections of the practice by the number of active patients. If the figure falls within $285 to $385 and the seller is claiming a typical clinical mix for a general dentistry practice, the active patient count is likely to be relatively accurate. However, if the figure is larger, say $725, and the seller is claiming to perform the run-of-the-mill mix of dentistry through the practice, the implications are that either the active patient count is inaccurate or the seller is doing a larger amount of higher cost dentistry relative to all other clinical work than he or she was aware of or is willing to admit. In either case, you should redouble your efforts to get a clear picture of the active patient count of the practice.

The practice's appointment schedule should also be checked for cancellations, activity level, weeks booked ahead, recall system, and new-patient count per month.

• *Third, Evaluate the Staff*
How long has the staff been with the practice, and is anyone leaving soon? Are any members of the staff related to the selling dentist? Look at all aspects of the pay. The gross wages of the staff are typically 22% to 28% of total gross production. Before your first day in practice, you should be thoroughly aware of the vacation/health/pension benefits and bonuses that the practice has historically provided. Then make a decision regarding which benefits you will provide.

You will be well served by going through an employment interview with each employee. Clearly, you will want to keep the staff intact, but these interviews will provide three big benefits: You will get free practice doing employment interviews (which will eventually come in handy); the staff will get a chance to meet the new owner up close and personal; and you will have the opportunity to learn about the systems in the practice from the perspective of its staff. The people and the systems determine the efficiency of the practice.

In evaluating staff, you should make note of their individual strengths and weaknesses. Every employee brings both to a position. However, some employees are much better suited for specific responsibilities than others, and very often an employee may be in a position that is not playing to his or her strengths. Buyers who conduct this staff evaluation carefully are positioned to take the helm of the practice and make the most of the strengths of the staff (which may include a realignment of duties several months after the acquisition transaction is closed).

• *Fourth, Evaluate the Facility*
Changes are often needed to make the operatories more efficient. Paint, carpet and furnishings need to be in good condition or should be replaced, repaired or just cleaned up shortly after the practice is acquired. Therefore, if required, you should carefully calculate how much money is needed so this amount can be added to the practice acquisition financing request, or considered in any further discussions regarding the price to be paid for the practice.

Dental Practice Receivables: Take Them or Leave Them?

One of the usual decisions to make when buying a dental practice is whether to acquire the accounts receivable (ARs) — those bills for dental services rendered that will not have been collected before the practice changes hands) as part of the transaction. The ARs are not purchased by the buyer in the great majority of dental practice acquisitions. Why, and what are the implications of either course of action?

Tax Considerations

The selling dentist pays taxes on the ARs regardless of whether they are included in the practice transaction. If you purchase the receivables as the new owner, the seller immediately pays tax, at the ordinary income tax rate, on the monies received. If you do not purchase the ARs, the post-closing flow of collections from the receivables are taxed as ordinary income to the seller in the year(s) in which the monies are received.

Why is there no tax liability for the buyer, either at closing or when the receivables are collected, when the ARs are included in a practice acquisition? It is because the money collected represents liquidation proceeds on an asset that was purchased. On the books, the collections on purchased receivables are recorded as income; they are then offset, dollar for dollar, by a write-off up to the value paid for the ARs.

Collections on ARs Purchase	$ 40,000
Collections on Post-Closing Production	$ 60,000
Gross Receipts	**$ 100,000**
Write-Off of Collections on Purchased ARs	$ 40,000
Post-Closing Operating Expenses	$ 80,000
Total Expenses	**$ 120,000**
Net Income (Loss)	**$ (20,000)**

Working Capital in Place of ARs

When you purchase receivables with the practice, you can count on an immediate flow of income to help offset expenses until your own production starts generating significant receipts. However, when ARs are not part of the purchase, you must borrow working capital or invest personal savings to cover expenses during the first month or two of your new ownership, which typically is how long it takes for collections on a new dentist's production to catch up with expenses.

Collections on ARs Purchase	$ -
Collections on Post-Closing Production	$ 60,000
Gross Receipts	**$ 60,000**
Write-Off of Collections on Purchased ARs	$ -
Post-Closing Operating Expenses	$ 80,000
Total Expenses	**$ 80,000**
Net Income (Loss)	**$ (20,000)**

Collections Risk vs. Reward

When purchased, ARs are bought at a discount since a collection rate of 100% is virtually impossible to guarantee. Therefore, buyers, and in particular their accountants, tend to worry a great deal about matching the discount for which the ARs are purchased with the actual collections they will experience on those accounts.

Much of this worry is unfounded. The collections rate on the receivables of most dental practices is very stable and easy to see in historical Production and Collections Reports and Accounts Receivable Reports. Thus, you could make a relatively informed offer to purchase the ARs of the seller at a discount that would most likely result in no loss of value for the ARs purchased. And if you are able to negotiate a preferential discount from a motivated seller, you might realize a nice gain on the purchase of ARs (note that the amount by which the collections on purchased ARs exceed the price paid for them will be recorded as income).

Despite this, many buyers decide not to take the risk, given the uncertainty as to the outcome of collections and that working capital financing offers a secure and predictable route to take. The scales are further tilted in favor of using working capital financing by the fact that the amount of money needed to meet the expenses of the practice in the first couple of months while the post-acquisition gap between production and collections is bridged is often less than the total cost of purchasing the ARs from the seller. Therefore, the buyer who opts to purchase the ARs will typically end up borrowing more money for the practice acquisition transaction than really is needed.

Other Issues

Buyers and their counsel have voiced concerns about the assumption of the billing habits, problems, issues and the like, of a seller through the purchase of his or her receivables. Buyers have argued that by securing working capital financing and leaving historical ARs to the benefit of the dentist who produced and billed for them, they are in effect placing a firewall between the pre- and post-acquisition billing and treatment activities of the practice. Put more bluntly, they believe that by leaving the ARs to the seller and using invested or borrowed working capital, they protect themselves from exposure to any pre-acquisition billing shenanigans and/or patient treatment practices of the seller.

Another thought voiced by some is that given the relatively complex nature of the negotiations and documentation required in a dental practice acquisition transaction, the addition of issues arising out of a decision to purchase ARs may serve to further complicate the process.

In the final analysis, the choice between taking or leaving the ARs in a dental practice acquisition generally is driven largely by personal perceptions rather than quantifiable dollars-and-cents reasons. Therefore, the ultimate decision may well rest with the buying dentist's tolerance for risk in hopes of gaining a larger reward.

CHAPTER 3

Role of Dental Practice Brokers

In most life situations, people use specialists to help them obtain the information or services they need. People go to their dentists to obtain dental care. They seek the services of insurance agents to help design an insurance program to meet their needs. They look to financial planners to help them obtain the financial security they desire. The list can go on and on.

Today, prospective buyers and sellers across the country are using the services of specialists who appraise and broker dental practices. Knowledgeable and experienced practice brokers are able to guide their clients through the complex problems associated with practice transitions and to ensure their clients' interests are well represented. Buying or selling a practice is one of the most important decisions of a dentist's career, so it is essential to have a broker with great integrity, good business judgment and a high degree of competency.

Practice brokers also can provide invaluable assistance when a dental practice owner wants to bring in partners through a fractional sale or when a dentist becomes disabled or dies.

Selecting a Practice Broker

A capable practice transition specialist must be well versed in a variety of different areas, such as:

- Proper appraisal methods
- Fair and effective sales techniques
- In-depth knowledge of the legal and tax implications incidental to the practice sale

Questions you can ask your practice broker to determine his or her competency include:

- Would you give me names and telephone numbers of sellers you recently represented?
- Could you explain to me the tax implications of the practice transition (especially if it involves a corporate practice and/or real estate)?
- How many practice transitions have you participated in during the previous two years?
- Can you describe for me the practice sales process from start to finish?

Practice Broker Assistance to Buyers

Most dental practices are sold with broker assistance, so serious buyers will want to get in touch with a broker active in the markets where they want to practice. Brokers typically work in limited geographical areas where they have a unique familiarity and understanding of the local dental market. They charge a commission or fee, which is paid by the seller, for the sale of the practice. With the advent of the Internet, a dentist can shop broker listings of practices all over the nation. There also are listings of practices for sale in *Dental Economics* and other major dental industry periodicals, as well as in local dental association publications.

To reach the point where a formal offer will be made on a practice, a good deal of work generally needs to be done to identify a target practice, determine its suitability, and come up with a purchase price offer. Once these steps are complete, the work continues as the formal offer to purchase must be delivered via an intent-to-purchase agreement, and upon the seller's acceptance of the offer, the buyer must conduct due diligence. The final two steps in the practice acquisition process are the drafting and negotiation of a practice purchase agreement (details of the purchase price and its allocation among the various assets of the practice, method of payment, the desired process/steps for transitioning control of the practice, obligations and duties of the buyer and seller, etc.), and the actual closing of the practice sale.

Clearly, before a prospective buyer does any of this, he or she would be well served to engage the services of a practice transition specialist, as well as an attorney and an accountant, to provide expertise, assistance and support.

Practice Broker Assistance to Sellers

It is often enticing to attempt to sell a practice on one's own. Superficially, the transaction seems simple enough, and a quick and easy way for the selling dentist to save money. Certainly, a few dentists have completed a "FSBO" (For Sale By Owner), but most have not. In fact, most FSBO transactions have occurred at a great cost in terms of the seller's time and the practice value realized.

Some key values a broker will bring to the sale of a dental practice are:

- *Valuing the Dental Practice Properly*
  It is easy to make the mistake of underestimating a practice's value and sell it for less than its fair market value or overvalue it and render it an unsalable asset.

- *Maximizing the Value Received for the Practice*
  Since the best brokers have been involved with hundreds of transactions, they know and can advise sellers to employ the best and most effective negotiating tactics.

- *Saving Sellers 10% to 20% in Taxes*

A critical issue in the practice sale will be the allocation of the purchase price for tax purposes. A seasoned broker will identify and implement strategies to save the seller significant tax dollars. Tax savings increases the net proceeds from the sale.

- *Cultivating a Larger Pool of Buyers and Generating Interest in the Practice*

Nothing has value without demand; therefore, a broker will create "demand" for the practice. This allows the seller greater leverage in negotiations. Practice transition marketing tools are either unavailable or economically unfeasible for most dentists. A broker enables the seller to take advantage of economy of scale.

- *Getting the Deal Closed*

Two dentists who spent years trying to sell their practices on their own complained about "too many tire kickers." Neither one had ever sold a practice, and they had a difficult time distinguishing and screening out qualified buyers from the tire kickers. Moreover, when a qualified buyer came along, they didn't know how to put the transaction together. The result was months of frustration. Finally, they each hired the same practice broker who sold both practices in less than six months.

- *Speeding Up the Process*

On the surface, the sale of a practice does not appear to be time consuming. Often, the selling dentist assumes selling the practice will be just like selling a home. Nothing could be further from the truth, as it is a much more complicated and involved transaction. A home is primarily structure and location. In addition to structure and location, a dental practice includes the dynamics of an ongoing business, staff members, a practice philosophy, equipment, supplies and patients.

Successfully delivering a smooth practice transition takes expertise, effective tools, experience, patience and hard work. It is an extremely time-consuming process that has tried the patience and resources of many dentists who have attempted to do it on their own. Clearly, it is difficult to measure empirically the value received by the seller through the amount of time and frustration a professional practice broker absorbs, but the value is real and not insubstantial. Proof is seen in the fact that there are busy practice brokers all over the country.

Practice Broker Assistance in Support of a Fractional Sale

A fractional sale is when the owner sells a portion of the practice to another dentist who will ultimately buy the remainder of the practice at an agreed-upon point in time in the future. Fractional sales are more complex than an outright sale in many ways. A practice broker can provide support for these transactions in such ways as these:

- *Marketing*
- *Screening of Candidates*
- *Valuation of the Practice*
- *Determination of the Amount of Ownership/Equity to Be Sold Initially*
- *Development of Financial Models*
It is very important in a fractional sale that the broker provide financial models that help to demonstrate the ability of the practice to support both parties, as well as the projected growth in the practice and the return on investment for the prospective buyer/partner.

- *Funding and/or Development of the Purchase Framework*
A portion of the purchase price often will be paid via a promissory note held by the seller. In these cases, the rate and terms of the note will need to be negotiated. Many buyers may request a structure that enables the use of pretax payments. Different payment structures add a level of complexity best handled by an experienced professional broker and CPA.

- *Development of the Buyout Formula*

The formula or methodology for determining the price to be paid for the remainder of the practice to be determined at a point in the future is important. Many prospective buyers do not want to be in a situation in which their contribution to practice growth creates a higher buyout price for them in the future. This can be addressed by using a formula or methodology established in the initial sale instead of waiting for the sale of the final portion of the practice.

- *Establishing the Basis for Distribution of Net Profits*

This is typically based on ownership; however, variations can be utilized.

- *Establishing the Basis for Compensation of the Joint Owners During the Partnership*

This is typically done through a combination of pay based on the individual dentist's production/collections, plus a split of the remaining net income according to the percentage of practice ownership.

- *Liaison with Outside Advisors and Attorneys in the Preparation of Legal Documents*

- *Overall Facilitation of the Process*

Practice Broker Assistance When a Dental Practice Owner Has Died

When a dental practice owner has died, a practice broker will immediately:

- Appraise the practice to determine its value, and justify that value to potential buyers and their lenders

- Request a real estate appraisal if the deceased dentist owned the building in which the practice is located

- Enter into a listing agreement with the personal representative or executor for the deceased dentist

- Recruit temporary dentists to operate the office while it is being sold
- Assist the spouse, if desired, in drafting a letter to send to all active patients
- Contact those dentists who are known to be in the market to purchase a practice
- Implement a comprehensive marketing plan to seek out additional qualified buyers

CHAPTER 4

Practice Valuations

To the owner, it may seem nearly impossible to put a price tag on the results of the hard work and careful planning that go into building a practice. However, this is the everyday job of specialists who appraise dental practices and work with prospective buyers or sellers.

The Practice Valuation Process

- All appraisal approaches are based on the premise of reasonable alternatives
- No single method is universally accepted by all appraisers
- No single approach or method is used in all instances by any one appraiser
- Practice valuation, like dentistry, is an art and a science

A current practice valuation is obviously needed when a practice is being prepared to put on the market. There are a number of other situations where it comes in handy. Knowing the real value of the practice is important for planning ahead for expected events like retirement, but is also vital when preparing for unexpected events such as divorce, disability or even death.

Dental practice brokers use a variety of methods to determine the value of a practice. Understanding the fundamentals of valuation can help you maintain — and increase — the value of your practice over the years.

Why Are Practice Valuations Conducted?

Here are the most common reasons why dentists will want and need to know the value of their practices:

• *Financial and Estate Planning*
Many advisors recommend a practice valuation so that dentists can integrate the value of the practice into their estate and retirement plans. A periodic/ongoing practice valuation can help determine if these plans are on target.

• *Associate Buy-In or Buyout*
Few dentists properly prepare for associate buy-ins or buyouts. Further, at a time when associates are very difficult to find, it is more critical than ever that such transition plans be in writing and include a documented present and transition date practice value.

• *Selling Parts of the Practice*
One of the myths in dentistry is that a large practice cannot be sold. In fact, a large, healthy practice is extremely attractive to buyers, and allows the owner the option of remaining on as a partner or associate.

• *Ready to Sell It All*
For those dentists who are ready to sell their practice ("lock, stock and barrel") now, the first step is to establish its value. The sooner the value can be established, the faster the practice can be sold.

• *Divorce*

In the unfortunate circumstance of a divorce action, the practice valuation should be prepared by someone with specialized knowledge and expertise in this area. An attorney or accountant might not have the industry knowledge to correctly evaluate the practice. If a person with dental expertise does the valuation, it will have a greater chance of being accepted by both parties to the divorce, and/or a judge.

• *Disability or Death*

Why not plan for the unexpected? Too often, dental practice valuation experts are called much too late in the game to help a dentist who is disabled or the spouse of a deceased dentist. If a valuation is prepared in advance and updated on a routine basis, many of the pitfalls of practice transition due to death or disability can be avoided. By establishing a practice's value and selecting a qualified practice broker or consultant to sell it in the event of premature disability or death, dental practice owners will gain peace of mind for themselves and their families.

Practice Valuation Methods

Accurately assessing the value of a practice involves utilizing several different methods. The three approaches most often used are the Market Approach, the Asset Approach and the Capitalization of Earnings Approach. These same approaches are used in the commercial real estate business under the names Market Comps, Replacement Value, and Income Value. Most dental practice appraisers use these approaches in combination, examining the current market for the practice (Market Approach), the value of the assets of the practice (Asset Approach), and the value of the practice as an ongoing business concern (Capitalization of Earnings Approach) to ensure that the ultimate value assigned to the practice is vectored from three established points.

There is also a simple method — the Rule of Thumb — that is sometimes used, although it does not provide the degree of accuracy that a seller or buyer would truly want when it comes time to seal the deal. According to the Rule of Thumb, if a practice's annual collections are, for instance, $300,000, then the practice is worth $300,000. No more, no less. Let's look at this method first.

Rule of Thumb Approach

This approach to establishing value as a multiple of practice collections is a very simple and speedy method of valuation. In other words, the Rule of Thumb Approach does not take into consideration, the local market size, mix or conditions; equipment condition/age; or the clinical/financial operating reality of the practice being valued. Therefore, by placing a value on a practice based on a simple Rule of Thumb, the owner/dentist runs the risk of either overvaluing or undervaluing the practice. A dental practice is made up of many complex elements. All of these components should be taken into consideration when valuing a practice.

---

30 Years Ago Practice Market Value Was Set by Rule of Thumb

- Rule of Thumb methods do not work well for any given practice, much less all practices
- Value is the result of multiplying the most recent year's revenue by a percentage, typically 50-80%
- Popularity is due to its simplicity, not its reliability
- Does not take into account cash flow, terms, location demand and many other important factors

---

Practice appraisers and brokers are often asked what they look at when they value a practice. The two key elements that receive the most attention are:

- *Tangible Assets*

It is easy enough for a dentist to get a value for equipment, leasehold improvements or supplies from either an appraiser or an equipment/supply company.

· Intangible Assets

The intangibles are more difficult to value. Such factors include location, telephone numbers, parking, accessibility from major streets, quality of patient base, quality of staff, organization of office systems, number of competing dentists in the area, fee schedule, financial arrangements, and size and appearance of the office and building. These factors, combined with many others, make up the "goodwill" value (e.g., the economic or ongoing concern value) of a practice.

To illustrate the impact that factors other than the size of a practice's collections have on the value of the practice, consider two practices recently sold:

- Practice A had gross collections of $216,649 during the previous 12 months.

- Practice B's gross collections were $218,802 for the same time period.

Based on the notion that a practice is worth a fixed percentage of gross collections (the Rule of Thumb Approach), both sellers should have received approximately the same amount for their practices. The practices were not sold for the same price, however.

Under previous ownership, Practice A had approximately 200 fewer active patients than Practice B, but Practice A was enjoying the influx of 14 new patients a month compared to only six by Practice B. Also, the potential in Practice A seemed higher, with the latest census reporting growth up 12% in its market compared to a 1.5% decline in Practice B's neighborhood. The value for patients varies considerably from practice to practice because of differences in patient profiles. Such things as age of patients, the proximity of their homes to the dental office, dental IQ (recall effectiveness), crown-and-bridge acceptance, paying habits, percentage of patients with insurance, and percentage of medical-assistance patients are all variables that prospective buyers consider. Based on the profile of patients in Practice A, the buyer was willing to pay $28 more per active patient than the buyer of Practice B.

The size and utilization of the offices differed in that Practice A had three operatories with room for a fourth in a 1,250-square-foot space, whereas Practice B had only two operatories and no room for expansion in a 580-square-foot area. Practice A also had a private office, a staff room and a full-time hygienist, while Practice B employed a hygienist three days a week. Practice A is located in a highly visible/popular strip mall, and Practice B is on the fourth floor of a large professional building. The appraisal of equipment and furnishings at fair-market value was higher in Practice A: $42,500 compared to $17,200 for Practice B. In addition, Practice A was computerized, whereas Practice B utilized a service bureau for its patient billings.

Given all of this, it should come as no surprise that Practice A and Practice B sold for different prices, even though their annual gross collections were basically the same. Practice A sold for 93.7% of gross receipts or $56,000 more than its counterpart at 67.2% of gross receipts in a market where the same prospective buyers looked at both practices.

Clearly, a careful comparison of the market value of the furniture, fixtures and equipment, historical practice and local market growth, office size, expansion possibilities, patient profiles, and location of these two practices showed they had less in common than their annual collections results would suggest.

Despite its shortcomings, the Rule of Thumb Approach to practice valuation is not without its merits, as it represents a relatively cost-free and generally effective method for making a rough estimate of value. If this method is used, most dental practices with a concentration of their collections coming from fee-for-service billing and located in highly populated metropolitan, suburban and urban markets are best valued by multiplying total collections by 75%. Meanwhile, most capitation and rural market practices will have their values best estimated by multiplying collections by no greater than 60%.

Asset Approach

Simply put, this approach attempts to apply a value to each of the individual assets that come together to make up a dental practice. It is quite subjective and by itself could, and does, generate much debate as to the accuracy of the value assigned to any given asset. However, if used in the context of a practice valuation that is considering several viewpoints of value, it is very useful in identifying and segmenting the value of individual assets in the practice. Once an offer to purchase is accepted, the value noted for practice furniture, equipment, supplies, etc., through the Asset Valuation Approach is often used to allocate the price paid for the practice for tax purposes.

Asset Approach

- What are my things worth?
- A very subjective approach
- Many times the outcome depends on who hired the appraiser
- Difficult to accurately appraise hard assets
- Valuation of intangibles can be extremely subjective

Asset Approach

Dental instruments	$ 5,000
Dental supplies	$ 6,000
Office furniture and fixtures	$ 9,000
Dental equipment	$ 80,000
Covenant not to compete	$ 50,000
Patient records	$ 25,000
Goodwill	$ 125,000
Total	**$ 300,000**

Market Approach

Often called the Market Comps (short for comparables) Approach, this approach simply compares the practice with other similar practices that have sold to determine its value. This is done by dividing the gross receipts of several similar practices recently sold by the price for which they were sold. The resulting percentages — for example, 75, 65, 72 and 74 — are then used to determine a percentage by which to multiply the practice's gross receipts and determine its Market Comp value. The theory behind this method is that the value of the practice is equal to that which other ready, willing and able buyers have offered and sellers have accepted for similar practices.

By itself, this approach has one major weakness in that it does not give adequate consideration to the qualitative and quantitative nuances of one practice versus another. However, here again, its greatest strength arises when it is used as just one of several approaches to determining value, as it gives credence to the value of the "potential" in a practice that every reasonable buyer will look for and consider when making an offer to buy.

Market Approach

- Compares the price/gross ratios of other similar practices that have actually sold
- Does not take into account terms
- A very powerful influence of price
- Price/gross ratios are easily evaluated on a scattergram

Income Approach

This valuation method seeks to determine the risk-adjusted present value of the future income one could receive as owner of a given practice (the value is adjusted for the risk that the income may or may not continue into the future and for future inflation). This approach is more complex than the Market and Asset Approaches, and it is one of the most important processes in vectoring in on practice value, as it is based largely on the income a practice has and may continue to generate.

Income Approach

- Price is derived from buyer's ability to pay overhead, debt service and earn a successful personal net income from the existing practice gross
- State-of-the-art approach for determining fair market value
- Used by better appraisers and preferred by accountants and lenders

The most common and reliable documents used in this valuation exercise are the historical tax returns of the practice to be sold. The income reported in the tax returns for the practice is adjusted — that is, either increased or decreased — for various historical expenses of the practice that were either understated or overstated for tax reporting or some other purpose having little, if anything, to do with the delivery of dental care.

Some of the most common upward adjustments to practice income in this process involve the add-back of non-cash expenses, such as depreciation and amortization expense and various elective/discretionary expenses benefiting the owner/dentist, such as interest, travel, entertainment, auto and pension/profit-sharing expenses. Clearly, none of the non-cash expenses or discretionary expenses are necessary for a dentist to produce billable dental services.

	2006	
	Tax Stmt.	% Recpts.
Hygiene Receipts	$ 200,000	20.00%
Dental Receipts	$ 800,000	80.00%
Total Receipts	$ 1,000,000	100.00%
Practice Overhead	$ 775,000	77.50%
Net Income	$ 225,000	22.50%
Adjustment		
Depreciation Exp.	$ 15,000	1.50%
Entertainment Exp.	$ 3,000	.30%
Interest Exp.	$ 5,000	.50%
Excess CE Exp.	$ 1,500	.15%
Auto Exp.	$ 3,500	.35%
Owner's Comp.	$ 175,000	17.50%
Owner's Comp-30% of DDS Receipts	$ (240,000)	-24.00%
Total Adjustments	$ (37,000)	-3.70%
Discretionary Income	$ 188,000	18.80%
Discount Rate	0.250	
Practice Acid Test Value	$ 752,000	

Instances where reported income is adjusted downward (by way of an increase in expenses) include, but are not limited to, situations where owner-occupied real estate results in lower-than-market office rent expense being assessed to the practice, or where family members work in key positions in the practice but their wages are reported at below-market rates.

An additional common downward adjustment to income results from the factoring in of compensation for the services rendered by licensed dentists. Often, no wage is expensed to the dentist/owner for services rendered when the practice is owned as a Personal Service Corporation, S Corporation or some other form of business allowing for the pass-through of income to the personal tax return of the owner, and just as often the wage expensed for the dental services of the owner is set at his or her personal income needs rather than some percentage of productivity. In the determination of practice value through the Income Approach, the expense for the wage of the owner/operator dentist is adjusted to a percent of collections generated by the dentist much like the majority of associate dentists are paid. A common percentage is 30% of dental collections.

The net result of these adjustments to reported taxable income can be termed "the income of the practice available to be used at the owner's discretion." This discretionary income is the key to determining the acid test value of the practice using the Income Approach.

At this point, the only real subjective element of this valuation process, the capitalization rate, is factored in. By dividing discretionary income by a percentage rate commonly referred to as the capitalization rate, a dollar value for the practice can be derived that takes into account the risks inherent in the practice and its historical cash flow available for the owner's discretionary use. The risks considered and thus embodied in the capitalization rate take into account a number of more qualitative aspects of the practice, such as the following:

- *Makeup of Income Coming into the Practice*
Income received in the form of fee-for-service payments for dental service rendered represents the least amount of risk to potential buyers for a practice. More risky sources of income to a dental practice include income received from capitation insurance plans and other discounted dentistry payors (including Medicaid) because, relative to fee-for-service payments received directly

from patient and from standard indemnity dental insurance plans, reimbursements for services rendered from these sources may not cover or continue to cover the base cost of delivering the dental care. The most risky source of income, in the context of a practice valuation, is that which is generated through the delivery of specialty dental services that few potential buyers may have the skill or training to provide (e.g., orthodontic or oral surgery services). During periods of local or national economic downturns, having large concentrations of a practice's income coming from the delivery of high-end cosmetic dentistry may be considered highly risky because of the potential for reduced discretionary spending by the patient base, resulting in a downward adjustment in practice value through an increase in the capitalization rate.

· *Quality of the Staff*
An experienced staff with a long tenure may be considered a plus compared to a new staff that lacks experience.

· *Growth Trend of the Practice*
If a practice is not growing, then it is dying.

· *Quality and Quantity of Equipment and Furnishings*
Is the equipment in good working condition and are the furnishings modern? Additional debt service expense may be incurred by the prospective buyer to bring the practice into compliance with the minimal current professional standards.

· *Visibility in the Community and Geographic Location Within the State*
Most purchasers want to be located in larger cities or medium-sized college towns with a lot of activity and good school systems. The least desirable, of course, are remote towns or areas with unstable economies.

When Value Meets Perspective

With all of the factors that go into the valuation of a dental practice, it is not surprising that buyers and sellers will have differing points of view regarding a practice's value. No sale can occur, however, until a compromise on value is reached, so the parties to these transactions are motivated to find common ground. Very often this common ground is reached less through movement up or down in the price of the practice and more through agreement on key structural elements of the transition.

The two most significant structural elements of a practice transition are:

• *How Will the Seller Be Paid?*
Options include all cash at closing, some cash at closing followed by monthly payments on a seller note, some cash at closing with the remainder paid depending on client retention once the practice changes hands, and some cash at closing with the remainder paid to the seller in the form of a monthly consulting fee or above-market rent.

• *What Is Being Purchased?*
Options include the assets of the practice, the stock of the practice, and the assets of the practice plus a consulting contract with the seller.

While the outcome of negotiations on these two factors can bring about agreement on value, consequent shifts in the tax payment obligations and the personal cash flow for both buyers and sellers after the sale can be significant. Buyers and sellers, therefore, should make sure that their personal accounting/tax specialists are involved in the negotiation of these aspects of the transaction in particular.

How Will the Seller Be Paid?

It is easy to see that if a seller receives cash at closing for 100% of the purchase price of the practice, his or her personal cash flow will be maximized. He or she will have liquidated the value in the practice and therefore, have the opportunity to live off the proceeds of the sale as needed. However, some sellers may be surprised at the negative tax implications of receiving all of their funds at the point of sale. They may be motivated to negotiate for the receipt of some portion of the sales price in installments following the sale. Such installments might involve monthly payments on a seller note, monthly consulting fee payments, or monthly payments of above-market rent for the practice's office space owned by the seller and leased to the buyer.

From a buyer's perspective, the decision on how to pay for the practice is driven by the need for enough cash flow following the acquisition to cover the overhead of the practice, his or her own living expenses, and payments on the practice acquisition loan. Chief among all elements that must come together to ensure sufficient cash flow is a smooth transition (defined as a transition where the level of historic production and collections are maintained).

In instances where the seller has been generating a tremendous amount of revenue through the delivery of high-end cosmetic dentistry or some other form of specialized dentistry such as orthodontics or oral surgery, a buyer will often perceive increased risk in terms of the likely difficulty in maintaining historic production and collections rates through transition. Buyers in this circumstance will often request some portion of the purchase price be paid by way of a seller note to ensure that the seller has ample incentive to support the buyer in maintaining the practice's historic level of production following the acquisition.

In instances where the agreed-upon purchase price is perceived as testing the limits of the practice's likely cash flow after the sale, a buyer may ask to pay some portion of the purchase price by way of above-market office rent or a monthly consulting fee. Both rent and consulting fees may be fully expensed and therefore, fully tax-deductible when paid, which would allow fully tax-deductible payments for practice value and ensure the seller's commitment to a successful transition.

Finally, in instances where the buyer and seller are at an impasse in negotiating a price for the practice, an "earn out" provision to the purchase agreement can bring about a meeting of the minds where no other solution seems to fit. An earn out provision simply notes that the seller will be paid, either in a lump sum or over time, some additional amount of money should the practice hit agreed-upon performance targets as measured at agreed-upon intervals. Performance targets often considered in earn out provisions are number of patients seen in a given period of time, production and/ or collection targets reached in a given period of time, and retention of specific specialty dentistry production. Some earn out provisions allow for an agreement on the larger purchase price at closing and call for downward adjustments if the agreed-upon performance targets are not met.

What Is Being Purchased?

The question of what is being purchased centers on the tax implications of the practice transition for both buyer and seller. In practice transitions where the transaction involves the purchase of the assets of the practice (typically classified as furniture, fixtures, equipment, and goodwill), the allocation of value between these elements can have a material impact on the post-closing tax position of each party, and consequently impacts the value they ultimately receive in the transfer of ownership. Furniture, fixtures and equipment are assets that, when sold, can result in a much higher tax rate for sellers than that paid on goodwill. Conversely, buyers receive a more favorable tax consequence from attributing as much value as possible to furniture, fixtures and equipment relative to goodwill, because those assets can be depreciated more rapidly than goodwill can be amortized.

Some ownership transitions involve the purchase of stock in the practice. Such purchases generally result in the seller receiving the best post-closing tax positioning and the buyer being left with one of the worst possible tax postures (the purchase price for the stock is not deductible as either depreciation or amortization, which results in the buyer being forced to pay 100% of the practice purchase price with after-tax dollars). Transactions of this sort still occur, however, as they represent a potentially effective method for "balancing the scales" in the process of achieving a compromise in practice value. In particular, because a stock sale allows the seller to recognize virtually the entire sales price (except for some amount attributable to a non-compete agreement between seller and buyer) as a capital gain, and pay less tax on the proceeds from the sale, an agreement on a lower purchase price may be achievable.

The transaction may involve the assets of the practice, plus a consulting contract with the seller in some cases. Consulting contracts with sellers offer buyers the opportunity to meet the seller's desired selling price with pre-tax income, as the full amount of each payment on the consulting contract is recognized as an expense when paid. For sellers, the implications of receiving payment for a portion of the value of the practice through a consulting contract are that the monies received will be taxed at the personal income tax rate of the seller at the time the money is received.

Opportunities for Practice Value Increases and Decreases

Just as lack of curb appeal may reduce the attractiveness of a home for sale, there are "little things" that can have a negative effect on the sale of a dental practice.

- *The Physical Premises*
  What would the office look like to someone who doesn't see it every day the way the owner does? Is the office clean and modern? Are the carpets clean and in good condition? Is the furniture inviting, or does it look like standard-issue, waiting room furniture? What does the receptionist's desk look like? Is it orderly, or are patient charts scattered everywhere? Is reading material current and neatly stacked? Are there current health care brochures, attractively arranged for patient browsing?

- *A Well-Organized Office*

Are records neatly filed and the front desk uncluttered? Is the office computerized? A visible computer in this day and age implies modernity and organization. How effective is the computer system? Is it being used as well as it could be for scheduling patients, keeping track of recall dates and maintaining financial records?

- *A Consistent Pattern of Growth*

Consistent growth as measured by annual collections indicates the strength of the practice and can reassure a potential buyer that the mechanisms are in place to help guarantee a successful future. A good benchmark for growth is 7% to 10% annually, or perhaps more if a good marketing plan is in operation. Strong new-patient flow is fundamental to generating growth in collections and is a key element in gauging the success of a practice.

- *The Mix of Patient Types*

Obviously, every practitioner would like all patients to be on a full fee-for-service basis, but it is seldom that way. Insurance, union plans and capitation have to be considered. Too high a percentage of patients on capitation or limited-fee HMOs can mean lots of work but little net profit.

- *A Friendly and Dedicated Staff*

A long-term, loyal staff provides a sense of permanence and stability. Patients feel much more comfortable visiting a practice where the staff is familiar, caring and obviously experienced.

CHAPTER 5

Seller's Guide

Whether it is for reasons of death, illness, disability, divorce, emergency family needs or simply retirement, nearly all dental practice owners or their estates will try to sell their businesses sooner or later. Unfortunately, most dentists wait until the last minute, or worse, never give serious thought to transitioning their businesses to new ownership. The consequences of this are the loss of practice value and consequent loss of income from the practice sale.

A practice has the most value when it is at its peak of performance. Without proper planning, many dentists find themselves trying to sell their practice during its decline, well after reaching its peak performance. With a proper transition plan, a dentist can achieve top value for his or her practice, and maintain and transfer that value to a new owner for a premium price.

Why Am I Selling My Practice?

The sale of a practice has to be one of the most important financial, personal and professional decisions that dental practice owners will make during their lifetimes. Therefore, it is equally important for practice owners to be able to answer the very important question, "Why sell?" Several common reasons why practices are sold include:

- I want to retire.
- I want to change careers.
- I want to relocate to a different part of the city, region, or country.
- I want to work for the buyer.
- I want to be a partner.
- The quality of the dentistry I provide to my patients is deteriorating.
- I have become disabled.
- I may die.

The reason is important because it will affect how the practice is marketed for sale, how the terms of the sale will be negotiated, and how successful the sale will be. The clearer a selling dentist is with regard to why the practice is being sold, the higher the likelihood the sale can be completed successfully. If you are thinking of selling but cannot write your specific reasons for selling down on a sheet of paper, you probably do not understand what you are trying to accomplish.

- If selling to retire, you should ask if this is the time to retire and why. Are you financially set for retirement? What will you do after you retire?

- If you want to sell the practice and work for the buyer, it is important to determine whether the practice is large enough to support two dentists. How will you feel about no longer being in a position of control? How long do you want to work for the buyer?

Many of the questions to be asked in this process are difficult to answer. Therefore, you should seek professional help from your accountant, financial planner, dental practice consultant, or dental practice broker experienced in practice transitions. It is also helpful to share your thoughts on the matter with trusted friends and/or other dentists who have sold their practices for the same types of reasons.

After going through this introspective process, a dentist should be ready to design and execute a transition strategy or identify a target date to develop a strategy. If you have achieved financial freedom, but you realize that there is nothing you would rather do each morning than go to the office, then a delayed or phased sale may be the best step for you.

The transition time of a sale can take anywhere from one to two years for a traditional retirement sale to 10 years for a partnership buy-in/buyout. It may require a minimum of five years if a dentist wants to "groom" the purchaser for a period of time prior to the transition. If the target date for total retirement is less than five years out, the options are a traditional retirement sale or working for the buyer after the sale, providing the practice is large enough to support two dentists.

Transition Time Matrix	
Retirement Sale	1 to 2 years
Pre-retirement Sale	1 to 2 years
Delayed Sale (A sale to an associate)	Minimum 5 to 10 years
Any form of co-ownership	Minimum of 10 years

Surviving the Trauma

After a lifetime of dedication to your patients, practice and staff, you need to live through the experience to really understand the emotional trauma of selling your practice. It is analogous to parenthood, in that, until you have experienced the birth of your first child, you simply cannot know the emotional impact of being a parent.

Many dentists who have sold their practices will ask themselves, "Why didn't I do this sooner?" They find that after years of the same work they are ready to make a change and move on. Some say they have enjoyed the time dedicated to practicing dentistry, but they have lost the passion and commitment.

While most dentists retire after selling their practices, many decide to change careers and have successfully moved on to new opportunities. Age does not seem to be a limitation when considering these other opportunities. Take the examples of these three dentists, all of whom created a financial and career plan with goals, committed to a change, and let go of fear. With the aid of experts, all three acted on their dreams.

• Dr. A decided to sell his practice and begin a new career as a CPA. Combining his dental and accounting skills, he established a successful affiliation with an accounting firm that had many dental clients. His firsthand experience and knowledge of dentistry enabled him to better serve his clients.

• Dr. B successfully merged his practice into the growing practice of a nearby younger dentist, freeing himself of ownership and management responsibilities. He reduced his time in the office with an option to cease practicing after the pre-determined target retirement date. With his free time, dentist B joined a dental consulting company and is helping dentists, young and old, in making decisions relating to transitioning their practices.

• Dr. C sold his practice and served as a department head at a dental school while pursuing a Masters of Business Administration. His background in private practice, combined with the business expertise from his MBA degree, made him a valuable resource for the dental school.

Start Now for Best Results

The reality of just what is involved in the process of selling a practice generally does not hit owners until the decision to sell has been made. Some of the doubts, realizations, and concerns that emerge following the statement "Let's sell it!" are as follows:

- Don't tell my staff.

- Don't tell my colleagues.

- Don't advertise the name of the town; someone might find out!

- You mean you'll tell Dr. X down the street that he can buy my practice? I don't think I want him to know how much I made and how much I charged.

- What do you mean it might take six to 12 months?

- No, I don't want to sign an exclusive practice brokerage listing; just work for nothing.

- You get how much of a percentage for brokering the practice? I know someone who will do it for free!

- Why do I need an appraisal? I know what my practice is worth!

- What is a proper practice appraisal going to cost me?

None of this anxiety and confusion is necessary, as there is no reason for dentists intending to sell their practice at some future date to wait until the last minute to realize and deal with this information.

Taking the following steps to prepare in advance will greatly reduce stress and increase your confidence as a seller. In addition, it is important to remember that planning and working in advance of the sale of a practice will contribute greatly to getting the best possible price.

Prepare a Game Plan for Selling Your Practice

A career in dentistry requires a written game plan defining the goals and objectives desired. These goals should include specific practice goals, personal goals, and financial goals. Things to consider in the plan include:

- Do I want a practice that is fee-for-service or managed care?

- Do I want to practice as a sole proprietor or be part of a group practice?

- Do I want to focus my practice on crown and bridge, cosmetic dentistry, TMJ, implants, family practice, etc.?

- Do I want a large practice or a small practice?

- How much do I want to make?

- At what age do I want to retire?

- How much money will I want and need to live on?

- Do I have adequate insurance to deal with disability, being out of the office for extended periods of time, malpractice, liability and death?

Align Fees

Fees should be evaluated and adjusted annually. Several resources are available to report treatment fees by percentile for a given zip code. Every dollar of collections flows straight to the bottom line. The income approach to practice valuation (see Chapter 4) determines practice value as a multiple of earnings. Therefore, if instituted soon enough, increasing practice fees to the norm can significantly add to practice value.

Do a Cash Flow Analysis

A cash flow analysis aids in determining the value of a practice. In valuing a practice, expenses are subtracted from income to determine net income. All expenses not necessarily related to the operation of the practice are added back to net income. The remaining adjusted net income must be large enough to make payments on the debt required to purchase the practice, and still provide for the wage needs of the purchasing dentist. The value of a practice cannot exceed the ability of the practice to pay all expenses, debt and a buyer's personal wage needs.

Maintain Production

Sometimes practice owners will start to slow down before actual retirement. This results in an exponential decline in profit and practice value. It is important to maintain the historic growth rate of the practice until the sale closes.

Keep New Patient Numbers Up

Purchasers focus on the number of new patients and consider it an indication of practice vitality.

Get Financial Records in Order

Most practice profit and loss statements or income statements fail to give a true picture of practice overhead and profit. You should ask your accountant to group related expenses together for the purpose of determining actual overhead and profit. All expenses benefiting you that actually are owner reimbursement should be grouped together. If two or more practices are involved, make sure to avoid a co-mingled tax return or financial statement.

Reinvigorate the Recall System

Hygiene receipts ideally comprise 20% to 22% of the total receipts in a typical general practice. This percentage can climb to 30% or more in practices aggressively utilizing soft-tissue management procedures. Generally, a higher hygiene percentage is better in terms of practice value. An exception to this rule is if the dentist is under-producing, which artificially raises the hygiene percentage.

Review the Condition of the Patient Records

In the due diligence process, a purchaser usually will review a representative portion of the patient records. You should maintain files with complete treatment entries, current patient information, and easily discernable treatment plans.

Clean Up Clutter and Spruce Up the Décor

First impressions matter. Most prospective purchasers will be looking at multiple practices. Every attempt should be made to make the practice stand out in the crowd, so you should invest in what it takes to maintain a fresh, updated office appearance.

Tune Up the Dental Office Equipment

Most purchasers expect to see modern equipment in the office. If they purchase a practice completely absent of modern equipment, they may adjust their offer to account for their anticipated need to replace outdated equipment. You should keep equipment updated, both functionally and esthetically. Beware of substantial replacement of the equipment just for the purpose of selling the practice, however, since this rarely warrants the full value of the investment.

Do Not Let the Office Lease Lapse

If the sale of the practice involves bank financing, be aware that the lender will require the purchaser to acquire an office lease with renewal options for at least the length of the practice acquisition note (typically ranging from 84 to 120 months). You should ensure that your office lease allows for the transfer or assignment of the lease.

Review the Treatment Mix

In a general dentistry practice, the performance of specialty dental procedures that cannot be easily duplicated by a purchaser can be a major obstacle in an otherwise routine transition. If specialized treatment (orthodontic, TMJ, implants, etc.) comprises a significant portion of the practice receipts, you should be prepared to be flexible regarding practice transition requirements and/or the price received.

Emphasize Fee-for-Service

Purchasers generally place a significant importance on the fee-for-service component of practice receipts. Practice owners should attempt to keep the majority of fee-for-service and carefully evaluate insurance plans they participate in. Make sure these plans can be transferred to another provider following a sale.

Work Closely With Advisors

Selling dentists should consult with their practice transition consultant about a preliminary practice evaluation. A good professional advisor will be able to point out any weak spots and make recommendations for correcting them.

Keep the Following Practice Information Up to Date

- Complete and accurate records that show charges, payments, adjustments and the profit of the practice for at least the past three years

- A list of employees, date of hire, hours worked, salaries, benefits and job descriptions

- OSHA records and manual

- A monthly breakdown of procedures by ADA code showing the quantity and dollar amount of each procedure for three years

- A current copy of the lease or information on the building in which the practice is located

- A written statement of practice philosophy and a policy and procedures manual

- A list of equipment, date purchased and amount paid at time of purchase

- A breakdown of practice income and expenses for the past three years

- A current count (done annually) of the number of active patients in the practice (active patients can be defined as patients who have been in the office at least once in the past 12, 18 or 24 months)

- The number of new patients seen in the practice monthly

- A description of marketing used to attract new patients

- Information on the geographic area where the practice is located

Have Periodic Practice Appraisals Conducted

It is a good idea to have the practice periodically appraised so that you will have some idea of what it might sell for. This is important information not only for you, but also for your estate planner, insurance agent, and those individuals who may have to sell the practice in the event of your death or disability. The key is to have a business relationship with a knowledgeable appraiser and/or broker who has sold practices in the area of the practice.

CHAPTER 6

Associateships and Partnerships

A successful associate relationship can be rewarding for both the practice owner and the dentist hired to work in the practice, and it is particularly rewarding when it results in a qualified and experienced successor for the practice. There are situations that can work against a cohesive relationship between owner and associate, however, and it is helpful if both are aware of the possibilities.

As with a successful associate relationship, a successful partnership relies on the compatibility of the individuals. It is important to find a good fit.

Creating Associateship Win-Wins

Owners generally want an associate to help with an overflow of patients; maintain or expand the days and/or hours that the practice is open for clinical care; generate revenue during times that the owner is away; and increase the profits of the practice. This said, a problem for owners today is that associates are not always easy to come by, and most want to be in upscale city or suburban areas. It's nearly impossible to find candidates for practices in rural communities.

Associates, though, interested in the business and clinical on-the-job training and the experience the position offers, are becoming increasingly interested in positions that lead to equity in the practice. Further, few new dentists interested in eventual ownership are willing to come aboard on the strength of a handshake and a promise that "One day, you can buy the practice." They want an all-encompassing agreement.

All too often, the hiring dentist and prospective associate leave their first meeting with a long list of unanswered questions, frustrations, and a feeling of dwindling confidence that is difficult to overcome. An old adage applies: "If you fail to plan, you plan to fail." The success of anything built or created depends on a solid foundation, so a practice owner wanting to add an associate should set the stage for a positive outcome by planning carefully from the beginning. In so doing, the hiring dentist will increase the appeal of the position, attract the best candidates available, and avoid entering a relationship doomed from the start. Prior to the first interview, employers need to do their homework. The following are steps that employers should take in preparing to discuss an associate position with confidence:

1. Complete a Practice Assessment
- Considering both short- and long-term demand for space, is the practice facility adequate for two dentists?
- Does the practice have the capacity or potential to meet the income expectations or needs of an additional dentist within a reasonable time?
- Are effective management systems in place and running efficiently?
- Is the practice overhead within a normal range (i.e., 55% to 60% of collections)?
- Is the practice collecting at least 95% of production?
- Is the staff open to change and completely committed to supporting an associate?

- Is the appointment schedule completely booked for a sufficient period?

2. Quantify the Financial Aspects of an Association

- Identify all fixed and variable costs related to adding an associate including staff, new equipment, instruments, laboratory, dental supplies, office supplies and expansion expense, legal, consulting, marketing, and associate compensation.

- Calculate break-even numbers for the identified associate costs with and without owner profit.

- Prepare short-, intermediate-, and long-term cash flow projections.

- Have the practice appraised if a future buy-in or buyout is anticipated.

3. Define the Basic Business Points

- *Relationship of the Parties*

Will the association be an employer-to-employee relationship or an owner-to-independent-contractor relationship?

- *Termination*

Delineate causes for involuntary termination and notice period for voluntary termination (covered in greater detail later in this chapter).

- *Compensation*

Compensation should be clearly defined. If compensation is based on a formula, it is typically a percentage of production or collections. If compensation is set as a percentage of collections, the associate agreement may include a draft against future earnings to provide the associate with income during the initial 20 to 40 days it takes for a full cycle of collections on billable treatment to be realized. Be prepared to offer an illustration.

- *Exclusive Service*

It should be determined whether the associate will devote all professional time to the practice, and whether he or she will work full time or be available only for a limited number of days or hours per week.

- *Records*

All patient files are typically owned by the practice and remain with the practice if an associate leaves, although post-employment access may be granted under specific circumstances and at the practice owner's discretion. Identify any exceptions to the general ownership and access provisions.

- *Expenses*

Outline who will be responsible for the cost of professional licenses, dues, continuing education seminars, health and malpractice insurance, benefit plans, dental and office supplies, laboratory expenses and staff salaries.

- *Time Off*

How many days will be allowed for vacation, personal time, or attendance at continuing education seminars? How much advance notice will be required for time off?

- *Covenants*

Restrictive covenants, such as nondisclosure of confidential information and non-compete clauses (with reasonable time and geographic limitations), are typically included in associate agreements. The subject of covenants is expanded upon later in this chapter.

- *Future Purchase Agreement*

Where an owner is establishing a relationship with an associate in view of a transition to ownership, he or she should be prepared to discuss how the buyout or buy-in price will be determined in the future and to offer a current practice appraisal and business points for a future purchase and partnership, if applicable.

Therefore, all the previously noted business points should ultimately be documented in an associate agreement. The associate agreement should also contain the method of compensation for services rendered, the length of the agreement, a restrictive covenant, responsibilities for lab fees and insurance premiums, independent contractor or employee arrangement, management responsibilities, whether it is intended that the associateship will eventually become some form of practice ownership and, if ownership is anticipated, a method for establishing the practice value at a designated time in the future.

It does not matter how much one party feels he or she can trust the other. Everything needs to be put into a signed, written agreement. Doing so will enhance understanding, expectations and ultimately the quality and success of the relationship.

Restrictive Covenants

One of the most critical elements of an associate agreement, from the standpoint of the owner, is a non-compete/non-solicitation covenant. For example, let's say an associate has worked in a practice for five years without such an agreement. During these five years of "seeing how things work out," the associate has, in effect, freely acquired the goodwill of the patients he or she has treated. Let's suppose the owner of this practice, which now has $1 million in annual collections, wants to sell and anticipates getting $750,000 cash for it. The collections are $500,000 on the owner's production, $200,000 on hygiene and $300,000 on the associate's. When the practice valuation is completed, the recommended sales price is only $500,000, or approximately 70% of the annual collections of the owner and hygiene. What has gone wrong? Why does a $200,000 gap exist between what the owner thought he or she should get for the practice and that which was determined by the practice valuation professional? The answer is that there is no buyer, buyer's accountant, buyer's attorney or buyer's lender who will support paying the seller for goodwill that actually belongs to an associate. The fact is this associate could leave with his or her patients and establish a new practice nearby.

Most practice owners in this position will initially attempt to negotiate an after-the-fact covenant-not-to-compete and a non-solicitation agreement with the associate. Unfortunately, this type of effort will be useless unless a payment is offered for this concession, and in some states such as California, non-competes and non-solicits are unenforceable on employees. So, is there anything this seller can do? He or she can absorb the risk for the value associated with the production of the associate by taking a note back from the buyer for that portion of the total purchase price. In this instance, let's assume that with the introduction of seller financing, the risk of the overall transaction for the buyer is reduced such that he or she agrees to pay the seller $750,000 for the practice. The seller and buyer enter into a $250,000 note to be paid over time, and the buyer pays the seller $500,000 cash at closing. If the associate subsequently leaves the practice and takes some or all of his or her patients, the typical provision in the practice purchase agreement and seller note would result in an automatic downward adjustment in the balance of the seller note to reflect the impact of the associate's departure.

Employee vs. Independent Contractor Associates

Another important issue is the status of the associate, whether that associate is an employee (W-2) or independent contractor (1099). Owners frequently will designate the associate as a contractor to avoid paying employer withholding taxes. The caution here is to ensure that the associate actually meets the criteria for a contractor. Does the associate provide his or her own dental equipment, instruments, supplies and auxiliary staff, and set his or her own schedule and work without any supervision? In such a case, the associate might possibly, but not necessarily, pass the contractor test. If these conditions are not met, the Internal Revenue Service may judge the contractor as an employee. The owner may then have to pay the IRS for all past withholding and payroll taxes, with possible additional penalties and interest. If the associate has been working for a year or more, this can become very expensive.

If the associate is incorporated, an owner may more safely consider contracting with the associate's corporation, and the associate's corporation will pay his or her salary and withholding taxes. Generally, if the associate is not incorporated, it is safer to regard that individual as an employee and withhold taxes and pay the payroll taxes due. These taxes amount to about 3% of the associate's gross production, so reducing the associate's commission by 3% would have the same financial effect as if the associate were a contractor who paid his or her own taxes. This avoids the huge financial risk the owner would face if the IRS disallowed a contractor status.

Termination

Regardless of efforts to provide for professional fairness, some associateships will make it and some will not. Many valid reasons for failure have been noted over the years, including inadequate compensation, insufficient patient flow, and lack of adequate written agreements. However, the most important prerequisite for staving off failure or realizing success in the employment of an associate dentist lies in the contractual provisions for termination.

Associate employment contracts should note the term of employment. They also usually provide for "cause" and "no-cause" premature termination of the agreement. These provisions allow the employer and associate to terminate the contract with a 30- to 90-day written notice. Reasons for termination for cause usually are straightforward. Examples include death or loss of license. Reasons for no-cause termination can be more arbitrary, such as, "I just don't want to do this anymore," or "Martha, my assistant, says you're hard to work with." Premature termination can be particularly harmful if the contractual "non-compete" clauses are not carefully crafted to protect both parties. Termination also can identify the end of one phase of the professional relationship and the beginning of the next; therefore, where an option to purchase is intended, it should be included and defined in the associate employment contract.

With that said, even in marriages, prenuptials only facilitate the breakup. Professional associateships are actually quite similar to marriages in terms of the emotional and personal feelings they can stir up. Therefore, it is logical to assume that premarital counseling during the courtship phase of the associateship will enhance the likelihood of a successful working relationship.

Employer/Associate Discord

Common causes of employer/associate discord include:

· *Money*
As with the breakup of most professional working relationships, the major reason for the failure of most associateships is money. In nearly every case where this kind of problem arises, one party feels he or she is not getting a fair share, and at the root of this conflict is the absence of a written contract. The value of an employment contract is seen in the order it forces on the parties to the contract as it is drafted, and the boundaries it provides during the course of the associateship. A well-written contract will clearly delineate the expectations and desired boundaries of both the employer and the prospective associate. With this type of document in place, both parties can move forward with a clear understanding of what is expected of them and, if necessary, negotiate for changes to the document within clearly delineated parameters.

· *Tight Financial Squeeze*
Owners often will pursue the employment of an associate before determining the ability of their practice to support more than one dentist. Most often this occurs in situations where the practice has experienced moderate to little growth in collections in prior years and/or is operating at the near-capacity of its physical space. If the owner moves forward with the employment of an associate under these conditions and does not invest in increased marketing for new patients and/or expand operating space, the associate will wither on the vine.

- *"I Got Mine, You Get Yours"*
Sometimes the owner dentist is generating sufficient collections
and has adequate space to accommodate the services of more
than one dentist, but is not willing to assign patients-of-record
or even new patients to the associate because he or she is not yet
ready to slow down and does not want to give up patients.

- *Personal Income Disconnect*
In some instances, the associate enters into the relationship
with an unrealistic expectation/need for income relative to the
position offered that could be easily dispelled by the seller at the
start, had the need been communicated.

- *Fundamental Character Flaw*
In some, but fewer instances, the owner dentist decides not to pay
the associate what had been agreed upon verbally.

- *Short End of the Clinical Production Stick*
Without an agreement addressing the matter, it is not uncommon
for associates to find themselves in charge of all of the managed
care and/or capitation patients, thus collecting a far lower
collections rate percentage per patient than expected.

- *No Written Plan*
When the plan is for the associate to transition into a position
of ownership, it is very common for sellers to change their mind
when a written document of the original understanding is not
in place.

Like in marriage, success of an associateship involves compatibility
between the parties. The best way to determine compatibility is
for both dentists to spend some time together prior to entering
into the relationship — preferably outside the dental office setting
— discussing dentistry and other important areas of life. Once
both parties find common ground for them to work together, it is
time to talk to a professional skilled in the crafting of associate
agreements.

Associateships in View of a Transition

It is important for owners who are interested in hiring an associate dentist, and ultimately selling him or her some portion or all of the practice, to achieve a meeting of minds prior to employment. The following steps are key to achieving this aim:

- Start the process when the practice is growing and thriving.

- Seek an heir apparent, not an associate.

- Seek candidates who have philosophies of patient care and management that are consistent with yours.

- Have open discussions with candidates about current and future plans.

- Differentiate your employment opportunity from others by updating and/or expanding the array of clinical skills and patient services offered through the practice.

- Prepare a written growth business plan to ensure the success of the associate candidate.

- Have a practice valuation prepared by a qualified expert to show the associate candidate that you are serious about the future practice equity opportunity being offered.

- Be prepared to discuss process, price, terms, tax allocation and transition timing.

- Seek out qualified advisors to integrate the accounting, management, financial plan and transition strategies.

- Monitor the transition process with frequent check-ins once the associate is on board.

- Include the dental team in the process on the front-end to ensure their future commitment to the practice.

- Be sure that the legal business entity suits the buy-in or buyout and ensures the proper tax consequences.

Associate Buy-In Timeline

There are three key phases in the associate buy-in timeline. Essential to making this timeline successful are, first, committing to action after the honeymoon period and, second, putting everything in writing up-front. Those two actions force both sides to honestly evaluate how the relationship will function in the future. There are creative ways to structure a practice buy-in. What works best depends upon the owner's particular practice situation. In any case, planning ahead, effective communication and written commitments will ensure the success of the practice transition.

Associate Phase

This is when the practice owner introduces a new associate into the practice. Two major periods make up this phase of the relationship.

Honeymoon Period

The purpose of this period is for everyone to get acquainted and determine if the relationship can be permanent. Each of the dentists should consider the compatibility of their respective practice philosophies. At the beginning of this phase, an associate employment agreement should be signed, production goals established, and a compensation formula agreed upon. In addition, a practice appraisal should be commissioned, the financial parameters of a future buy-in should be discussed, and a letter of intent should be drafted.

Commitment Period

At this stage (typically after a few months), the associate and the practice owner make a commitment to each other. A letter of intent detailing the buy-in terms is signed along with a practice-management agreement and any revisions to the employment agreement. The associate is accepted as a future partner. If the owner is bringing the associate on in order to ultimately retire from dentistry, a long-term plan to transfer patient records and referral sources is developed. What will happen in the event the senior dentist dies or becomes disabled during this phase should also be incorporated into the letter of intent. Typically, the associate agrees to commit to the buy-in phase as soon as the letter is signed. This way, both the senior dentist's estate and the associate's future interests are protected. The time frame for this period is typically six to 18 months. During this time, the legal sale agreement and other documents are prepared and signed. All arrangements, including the financial terms for the buy-in, are completed as early as possible so that everything is in place when the actual date arrives.

Buy-In Phase

The buy-in phase establishes what the practice is worth. If everything has been done correctly in the first phase, this will be effortless and seamless. In this phase, attention needs to be given to:

- Pricing
- Percentage of ownership
- Stock vs. asset sale
- Down payment
- Duration of financing
- Interest rates
- Tax considerations

Buy-ins are accomplished in some instances through some form of joint working relationship (for example, as joint owners of a partnership, limited liability company, S corporation, or C corporation). Such buy-ins may be relatively long in duration, with some lasting 20 years or more. In these cases, consideration should be given to:

- Control issues
- Division of administrative duties
- Decision-making
- Limitations on spending

- Partnership perks
- Division of income and expenses

Departure Phase

The final phase of a buy-in relationship will be the departure of the original owner. This phase will terminate the relationship that started with the associateship. The departure of the original owner can happen either involuntarily (death or disability) or voluntarily (retirement, third-party sale or dissolution). This phase involves consideration of:

- Events that trigger a buyout
- The structure of a buyout
- Down payment and financing
- Interest rates
- Deferred compensation agreements
- Tax considerations
- Dissolution stipulations
- Retirement requirements (e.g., notice, covenant not to compete)
- Disability definition
- Short- and long-term disability contingencies

Associate Buy-In Problems and Solutions

Well-informed parties entering an employer-employee relationship will always have the best shot at success. Even the best of plans and intentions will break down in some instances, however. The following are several rough spots that can grow into significant barriers if not recognized in advance and/or dealt with effectively as they arise.

Battle of the Generations

The typical age difference between the employer dentist and associate dentist is between 18 and 22 years. This means that they each come from two different perspectives. They were trained differently and likely have a different world view. These differences can be too great to overcome, but if they are, it will be done through regular communication. A plan of scheduled meetings outside of the practice where the employer dentist and associate can discuss real and perceived opportunities, concerns, etc., in a clear and respectful manner is critical.

Lack of Ownership Mentality

One complaint often heard from employers about associates is, "They don't look at problems or see opportunities in the practice the way I do." This comment is one that could be heard from business owners in any number of fields. How does a dentist get an employee to take ownership of events, processes and the ultimate success of the business the way an owner does? Is it reasonable to expect employees to achieve this level of attention to business matters?

For some employees, the problem is a general lack of interest or desire to do more than is absolutely required. The good news is that every business needs lots of employees who are happy doing what they do and not aspiring to be the head of the company. In most cases, however, associate dentists do care about the business and are intelligent enough to handle any and all aspects of it. The proof is that when dentists buy or start their own practice (as hundreds do each year), and join the real business world, less than 0.5% fail. This being the case, a likely solution to the problem of an associate's "fire in the belly" is to assign him or her the responsibility and autonomy to pursue the completion of several aspects of the management of the business of the practice. The employer dentist can then provide guidance as requested or needed and grow an increasingly competent and effective associate while better leveraging his or her own clinical or personal time.

There will always be some dental practice owners who worry that if they teach their associates how to run the practice, they risk losing them. The truth is that dentists are among the most highly skilled and mobile employees anyone in any industry can hire, and if they don't feel they are growing professionally or being treated fairly, they can and will leave (just ask the Monarch, Castle and other dental practice management companies about the difficulties in holding on to quality dental associates). Therefore, the best way to retain and groom associates and possible heirs apparent is to empower them and take the time to mentor them.

Not Enough Patients

Generally, a dental practice should have a minimum of 2,000 active patients and be growing by 15% per year before it considers bringing in a second dentist. An active patient is one who has received a service from the practice in the past 18 months and has not died or moved away. All too often, owners add associates when they are just slightly busier than they want to be, only to have the schedule ease off once the associate is on board. If there aren't enough patients, eventually both dentists will have difficulty filling their schedules. If this lasts for an extended period, the owner will begin to make less, and his or her relationship with the associate will be afloat on troubled waters.

Inability of the Practice Owner to Share the Sandbox

Most dentists practice alone because that's the way they prefer it. This is not a character flaw, but rather a fact of life. While most practice owners think they would enjoy the professional companionship of having another dentist in the practice, many don't enjoy the experience once the associate is hired. It is not easy to share patients, decisions about operations, and personal space. This problem can best be dealt with through personal introspection prior to the hire.

Failure of the Associate to Build the Practice

As noted earlier, associates are often brought in before there are enough patients to support more than one dentist. The reasons why this is sometimes done are twofold. First, some practice owners have never had to actively pursue new patients, and do not fully appreciate the difficulties and expense involved in marketing for the production capacity of two or more dentists. Second, some hiring dentists believe the mere presence of an associate and expanded office hours will generate the patient flow. Unfortunately, an owner's shortcomings in terms of bringing in needed new patient flow, whatever they may be, will not likely be offset by the efforts of an associate. Remember, it is most often the case that the associate is the sponge in the office soaking up business and clinical experience and skill. They, therefore, are not likely to lead initiatives such as increasing the new patient flow of the practice. Do not hire an associate until the patient base of the practice, including consideration for monthly new patient flow, can justify it.

Staff Conflicts

Problems between the owner and associate dentists often are centered around the employees of the practice. Sometimes, especially when the associate brings new ideas to the practice, employees do not like the change or extra work that comes with having a second dentist on board. The solution is to get the staff in sync with the idea of adding a new dentist and possibly allow several key staff members to meet with or interview associate prospects prior to extending an offer of employment.

Failure to Discuss Expectations

Most practice owners know what they want and what they like. Associates, like most employees, want to please their employer, but if they don't know what the hiring dentist wants and expects, their chances of doing this are greatly limited. Prior to bringing in an associate, the hiring dentist needs to take time to carefully walk through his or her expectations for the position and to share them with associate candidates prior to extending an offer of employment. Further, to meet the associate's need for feedback in order to stay on track, the hiring dentist should schedule several performance review meetings during the first year of employment.

No Clear Goal as to Buy-In

A majority of today's associate dentists have a strong desire to own a practice within three years of graduation from dental school, and are unwilling to labor for years without the chance of becoming an owner. Therefore, if the hiring dentist is convinced that an associate candidate is not someone he or she would want to be in partnership with, or if the hiring dentist has no desire to have a partner at all, it is essential that this be disclosed to the candidate as soon as either of these conclusions is drawn. The owner is the owner and, as such, reserves the right to change his or her mind. However, the honorable and best thing for both parties is for the facts to be put on the table as soon as they arise.

Unexpected Events

Despite the best of intentions, the best-laid plans of the employer or associate will go off track at some point. Derailments will occur as a result of family illness, a change in health or marital status of either of the parties, or any number of other life-changing events. There are likely to be as many solutions as problems that fall into this category; however, one clear course of action is to communicate the good, the bad and the ugly regularly.

Partnerships and Fractional Sales

The use of fractional practice sales or partnerships is growing in popularity as a transition strategy for owners who want to continue to practice past the peak of their individual productivity ability or interest. This involves the sale of a portion of a dental practice to another dentist who will ultimately buy the remainder of the practice at an agreed-upon point in time, based on an agreed-

Keys to Success

- Put everything in writing
- Maintain clear communication
- Determine how income will be split after the buy-in
- Determine how the total value of the practice will be divided when parties separate
- Determine what will result in a dissolution of the relationship
- Determine how to dissolve the relationship

upon method for determining buyout price, and who will jointly own and operate the practice in the interim. It is appropriate if the practice owner:

- Has an associate he or she wants as a successor
- Wants to share the responsibilities of ownership
- Wants to assure his or her exit strategy at some point in the future (typically at least five years out)

As with a successful associate relationship, a successful partnership relies on the compatibility of many factors between partners. However, adding a partner is a more complex process than adding an associate because of the element of immediate ownership, which means it is even more important to find a good fit. Experience suggests that for success in a partnership or fractional sale, the parties involved must:

- Be compatible in terms of their professional/clinical philosophies
- Be compatible in terms of their business philosophy
- Be compatible in terms of their overall vision for the practice
- Share a mutual respect for each other
- Be able to meet their personal income needs from the income of the practice

In the process of considering the addition of a partner, dental practice owners should ask themselves the following questions:

- *Is it a Good Idea Financially and Does It Support My Long-Term Financial Plan?*
Adding a partner will bring about significant financial changes for the owner and the practice. It may require a short-term decrease and, in a worst-case scenario, a permanent income reduction for the owner. Therefore, a practice owner considering bringing on a partner would be wise to meet with his or her financial advisors to discuss the financial implications of such a step.

• *Why Am I Doing It?*

Answers such as "My friend brought in a partner and it worked great for him" or "The seminar presenter told me I would be sorry if I didn't act now because I might not find a buyer later" are not good reasons. Some people should not have partners. Again, this is not a character flaw, but rather a fact of life. Time should be taken to really contemplate whether adding a partner is the right step to take.

• *Can I Share Patients, Decision-Making and Income?*

Most practice owners who consider bringing in a partner have practiced solo for many years and are not accustomed to sharing patients or management decisions. Others have had an associate for a number of years and have made a profit from the associate's production. Once the associate becomes a partner, the profit for the entire practice, including that derived from the hygiene department, is shared.

• *Do I Have an Active Practice?*

One telling sign is the number of active patients (patients seen at least once during the last 18 months and who have not died or moved away). As with associateships, one reason that partnerships fail is because there are not enough active patients to support two dentists. A practice needs at least 2,000 active patients and to be growing the patient base a minimum of 15% per year to support a second dentist.

• *Will My Facility Support Another Dentist?*

The answer to this depends on how the partners plan to schedule their time. If they plan to work the same hours, more operatories will be needed than if a staggered schedule is used. Generally, in a partnership of two dentists, the minimum number of operatories, even with a staggered schedule, is five.

• *Does My Practice Have Good Operating Statistics?*

Adding another dentist will only make matters worse if the practice is not growing and collecting what it produces. If there are problems filling one dentist's schedule, it will be impossible to fill two. Moving forward with a partnership with these types of problems would be comparable to a couple with marital problems deciding to have a baby in order to improve their marriage.

• *What Is My Practice Philosophy?*
It is amazing how many dentists have not taken the time to write a practice philosophy. For those dentists considering entering a partnership, it is essential for the practice philosophy that will permeate the practice during the partnership to be articulated in writing in advance.

• *What Is My Financial Philosophy?*
It is not unusual to have one financially conservative dentist and one financially liberal dentist practicing together. Guess what these partners argue about? Opposites do not function in a complementary manner in this matter, so a common documented financial philosophy is imperative.

• *What Are My Expectations for a Partner?*
When it is time to negotiate the buy-in and operating agreements, the partners should share their expectations and, as much as possible, these or some compromise should be included in the written agreements.

• *Am I Willing to Go Through the Process of Finding the Right Partner Several Times if Necessary?*
Adding a partner takes courage. When hiring an associate in view of a partnership or negotiating with a dentist to join the practice as a partner, the practice owner should do so with the understanding that he or she will walk away the moment the realization that the prospect won't work out occurs. Starting over can be expensive and frustrating, but getting out of a bad partnership is far worse.

Partnership/Group Practice Contract Considerations

In most transitions involving the sale of ownership interests within a partnership or group dental practice, the departing dentist receives a certain price, paid by the new dentist, for his or her part of the practice. Problems unique to group dental practice transitions can develop unless proper contractual provisions are included in group contracts involving employment issues and ownership issues. Some examples include, but are not limited to:

- How and under what conditions will terminations take place?
- How will the value of the practice of the departing dentist be arrived at under different situations such as death, disability, retirement, moving out of the area or staying in the area?
- How will the transition of the departing dentist's patients be handled?

This last example is important because there have been instances where the remaining dentists in the group have encouraged patients of the departing dentist to come see them. This has occurred because one or more of the remaining dentists treated some of the departing dentist's patients as an emergency or performed an exam on some of the departing dentist's patients while he or she was out of the office. The departing dentist also might have referred some patients to other dentists in the group for specific procedures. Whatever the case, loss of existing patients to other members of the group is clearly unfair to the buying dentist because he or she will not receive the value thought to be purchased. A relevant concern of dentists thinking of buying into a group practice is the retention of the patients of the selling dentist. A byproduct of this is that the new dentist may be unwilling to pay the asking price for the departing dentist's percentage of the group practice.

To deal with this, many groups have written into their group practice agreements what is referred to as the 85/15 rule. This rule states that if any patient of the departing dentist sees another dentist in the group before that patient has seen the buying dentist, the dentist whom they see must pay the buying dentist 15% of the gross production on those patients for a two- or three-year period. A variation on this rule is the 90/10 rule, which provides for a payout of 105% of the gross production on those patients for a four- to five-year period. Both the 85/15 and 90/10 rules serve to discourage other dentists in the group from pursuing patients of the departing dentist for their future dental needs by greatly reducing any profit they can realize on those patients relative to their own. In most instances these rules result in the other dentists in the group making every effort to encourage the patients of the departing dentist to see the new dentist. These rules also serve to reduce the new dentist's concerns regarding patient retention through the transition, and thus serve to support a full price payment for the departing dentist's percentage of the practice.

All existing and future dentists involved with group practices benefit from group contracts that clearly detail important codes of conduct, methods for addressing wrongs, formulas for determining value, and the like. It is important to obtain competent help before joining, starting or departing from a group practice so that all matters are covered in the agreements that are signed.

Partnership Pitfalls

Four pitfalls should be understood and considered before you enter into a partnership.

• *Loss and Absence of Control*
When a shareholder is reduced to or starts out with less than a majority interest, he or she is referred to as a minority shareholder. Being reduced to or buying into a minority interest is similar to owning a job, and dentists today are in sufficient demand that they do not need to pay for a job. Even a 50/50 arrangement results in both parties to the business relationship being minority shareholders, since neither shareholder has full control over any issue. Important issues can reach an impasse when neither party has the control to establish policy. Unfortunately, ultimate resolution to these dilemmas is the dissolution of the partnership,

which can be as contentious as a bitter divorce. It is natural for most dentists to want to own a majority interest, which means the other dentist must be willing to accept a minority interest.

• *Loss of Marketability*

Loss of marketability is another consequence of converting a practice into undivided interests through the creation of minority shares. An interest in a dental practice that is characterized as a "closely-held minority interest" is at risk of not being freely marketable, and thus not readily sold. By contrast, this is not the case with an interest held in a public company by way of its common stock, which is a marketable minority interest that is freely tradable and can be sold with the push of a button.

• *Loss of Value*

Loss of value can occur when a shareholder buys a minority interest. Too often, a dentist will seek an appraisal for a whole practice and then divide the price by two in order to price a 50% interest. This is not necessarily a true reflection of the value of this minority interest, however.

• *Shareholder Conflict*

Shareholder conflict often occurs as a result of all parties being subject to the same practice policies and structure. Each management decision will affect all shareholders universally. Decisions on pension plans, renting or building an office, staff, equipment, compensation, and the hundreds of other administrative details of managing a practice have the potential to raise controversy and ill will between the shareholders. The constant need for consensus increases the potential for conflict between the shareholders.

When a partnership goes bad, it can be one of the worst experiences a dentist will face. There are partnership dissolutions that have taken as long as three years to resolve.

The Solo Group – An Alternative to Associateships and Partnerships

As noted, prior to considering any form of associateship or partnership, a practice must have production sufficient for more than one dentist. For purposes of this section of the book, we will call this excess production the "Phantom Practice."

This is how the solo group alternative works: A dentist joins an ongoing practice under the terms of an associateship agreement for five years. The associate is paid a percentage of his or her collections, and agrees to a non-compete if he or she breaks the agreement or is terminated with cause. If the owner fires the associate without cause, the covenant is canceled. After five years, the employment contract ends and an office-sharing agreement begins. As a result of the development of the associate's separate practice, a solo group practice has been formed. Both practices share the common office and enjoy the economies of scale. With the exception of the death of one of the parties, the covenant-not-to-compete ends. (If a surviving party does not purchase a decedent's practice, a covenant-not-to-compete goes into effect.) Whatever practice the associate has developed during the first five-year period now belongs to the associate. The owner and the associate divide the total practice net income on a prorated basis of their individual production. If both parties produce the same amount of income, they are each paid the same amount.

This is a simple plan with the following profound benefits for both parties:

1. The original practice owner realizes greater financial gains than would be realized in a partnership through the accumulation of 100% of practice profits during the five-year associate period.

2. The associate does not have to pay a large price for an interest in someone else's practice in transition to ownership, thus eliminating any risk, debt or liability.

3. There is no discount in the value of the associate's practice, since the associate now owns his or her individual practice, not just an interest in someone else's.

4. Both the owner and associate can each individually manage, and even sell, their own personal practices or terminate the solo group arrangement with no lingering debt or litigation if the relationship does not work out.

All relationships will end — it is not about if, but rather how and when. With the solo group arrangement, the terminations have been simplified. This structure provides safety for both parties. The owner continues to maintain control and ownership, and therefore the marketability and value of his or her practice. The associate gains ownership and control of his or her individual practice without risk, debt or liability, while also preserving ownership, control and marketability.

CHAPTER 7

Smooth Transitions

The goal for both parties in a practice transition situation should be a win-win. The seller wants to be fairly compensated for the value of the practice while placing his or her patients and staff in good hands. The buyer wants to pay a reasonable price while retaining the goodwill and support of the seller in transition. The key is for both buyer and seller to identify and remain focused on what is most important and to be sensitive to the factors impacting the other party in the practice transition negotiation.

Respect, Dignity and Goodwill

In the negotiations surrounding a practice acquisition, it is normal for both buyer and seller to strive to obtain the best deal possible. It is critical, however, for the seller to depart the practice with a feeling of respect toward the buyer and with his or her dignity intact. The buyer has nothing if he has not obtained the goodwill of the seller. Therefore, in the transition of a dental practice, the focus must be on striking a balance. In this context, balance means the seller knows that he or she has left the patients and the practice in good and competent hands, and the buyer feels that he or she has maximized the goodwill transfer from the seller.

The best way to do this is for both the buyer and seller to view all matters being negotiated from both perspectives. Buyers and sellers would be well served to keep in mind that the practice sales process is stressful. Sellers are often stressed because they are retiring from the profession that has given them their identity. They are selling the manifestation of their years of education and labor, and leaving their business family (the staff). Buyers are stressed because they are making one of the most important personal and business decisions of their life. In most cases, the buyer is adding practice acquisition debt to $125,000 or more in student loan debt.

Elements of a Successful Practice Transition

Before the actual closing date, many important tasks need to be completed:

- The letter of intent, sale agreement, office lease and other documentation must be reviewed and approved by the buyer and seller, financial advisers and attorneys for both sides.

- The financing source also will have several documents that need to be reviewed and approved.

- Insurance including commercial liability, life, disability, practice overhead, workers' compensation and malpractice need to be purchased.

- Dental, business and state drug licenses all must be obtained. The NPI numbers, Federal Tax ID numbers, state and local tax-identification numbers must also be obtained. Dental insurance-carrier agreements and fee-schedule approvals must be in place if the practice accepts discount fee plans or capitation plans. A written OSHA plan and HIPAA statement must be written. If the practice will be receiving Medicaid patients, a Medicaid application must be filed and Medicaid number obtained.

Many dental practice buyers and sellers may think that the sale is complete when the sales agreement is signed, the check is issued, and the handshakes are completed. However, a successful transition calls for much more work.

The loyalty of the staff must be transferred from the seller to the buyer. Particular attention should be paid to the receptionist, as patients will pay attention to her enthusiasm for the transition. The receptionist will help allay any fears patients may have about the new dentist.

The seller must mail a well-written letter introducing the buyer to the active patients and referral sources of the practice. This is an important element in transferring patient loyalty. The letter can accomplish a lot if it is sincere (e.g., takes the patients' feelings and fears into account), and praises the buyer's character and background.

The Staff – To Tell or Not to Tell?

When it comes to selling a practice, the staff plays a critical role not only in the transfer, but also in maximizing the value of the practice and its ultimate selling price. The goodwill of the staff, especially the key employees, often can be more important than that of the seller from a purchaser's perspective.

Sellers frequently are reluctant to mention the possibility of a practice sale to their staff for fear of "spooking" them, even though the staff may sense it without being told. The selling dentist may want to keep the initiation of the sales process confidential. However, it is often impossible to prevent speculation if the seller is frequently receiving anonymous calls or behaving secretively. Therefore, it may be better to head off speculation and distrust by notifying the staff as early as possible and presenting the sale in a positive manner. When the seller addresses it this way, most staff members will likely respond in a positive manner and will appreciate their employer's forthrightness. Most staff members want and need to keep their jobs, so they may be more receptive than might be expected. Their favorable attitude will give the buyer a sense of continuity and help reduce the loss of valuable employees.

Once the seller has accepted a purchase offer, the staff can be brought in contact with the prospective buyer under the seller's supervision. Once the acquisition transaction is completed, a staff meeting should be called to order by the seller. The seller should start this meeting off by giving the new owner an enthusiastic welcome and a brief introduction. The seller should tell the staff why he or she thinks this particular dentist will work well with them and patients. Then, the new owner should take over the meeting. The new owner might start off by handing out a CV, showing family photos, and mentioning how he or she likes the area. In short, the buyer should create a friendly atmosphere and make the staff feel comfortable. The new owner should express a few of the reasons why the decision was made to buy this practice and make sure staff members know their value to the practice. Such communication could go as follows:

"I am very impressed with this practice, and I look forward to working with all of you. I'll be spending the next few months getting to know the patients and working with you. I can't possibly manage this office without your help and experience. We will have many opportunities to get to know each other and learn to work together. During this time, we'll be evaluating each other's performance and having a joint learning experience. This can be trying, so we'll have to be patient with each other. I'm not a dictator, but from time to time I'll be recommending office changes, which we'll discuss at our staff meetings. I need your input, and I promise I won't make any major changes without discussing them with you first. I look forward to working with you. I'm sure we'll develop a positive relationship and the practice will continue to be successful and grow."

The selling dentist should make it one of his or her highest priorities to see that the new owner and the staff quickly form a close bond. Doing so will assure the continuity of the seller's hard-built practice and help ensure that both patients and staff are comfortable with the new dentist who will take the practice into the future.

Will the Staff Stay?

The fear that existing staff will not stay with a new dentist is largely unwarranted in the majority of practice transitions. Although it could happen, it normally does not. Here's why.

When a new dentist buys an existing practice, staff members have two options:

- Stay on (provided the new owner asks) and continue doing their current jobs
- Leave and look for new positions in other dental offices

When the existing staff remains with the practice, they enjoy the advantage of:

- Maintaining their current salaries and benefits
- Retaining their seniority
- Knowing the other staff members and how they work
- Understanding the current office policies and procedures
- Knowing the patients

The disadvantages facing any member of staff who considers resigning and changing jobs are:

- A change in salary and benefits
- Loss of seniority
- Having to become acquainted with and learn how to work with a new staff
- Learning new office policies and procedures
- Learning how to use new equipment
- Building relationships with new patients
- Getting to know and learning how to work with a new dentist

If staff members remain with the current practice, they must deal with only one new variable, the new dentist. The impact of this variable is generally offset by the fact that the staff will still have to deal with learning the expectations of a new dentist if they leave. Staying with the existing practice is clearly far less of a gamble for staff. Here is a simple formula for retaining good staff.

- *From the Seller's Side*
Being sensitive to long-time, loyal employees is an extremely important element in a successful transition. These staff members should be taken aside and personally told of the pending change. This can be done immediately prior to the staff meeting where the seller announces the transition and introduces the new owner. The timing of this meeting varies with each practice transition.

- *From the Buyer's Side*
Staff should be assured that their jobs, salaries and benefits are secure and will not change. If the practice doesn't offer benefits, but the buyer plans to provide them, he or she should let the staff know about the new plans. The buyer would be wise not to lower employees' salaries or benefits, because this might prompt them to look for new employment. Buyers need to understand that the staff's anxiety level will be relatively high until they get to know the new dentist. In general, the buyer of an existing practice can assure staff retention by being sensitive, reasonable and treating staff members as he or she would like to be treated if the roles were reversed.

Transfer of Patients in Practice Sales

One of the greatest fears buyers of dental practices have is that the patients of the practice they are purchasing are going to "jump ship" and leave when the buyer takes over. Buyers frequently say, "Shouldn't I expect to lose one-third to one-half of the patients when I take over a dental practice?" The answer is: If the transition is done properly, there is no reason to lose anywhere near this many patients. The average patient loss after a dental practice sale rarely ever exceeds the typical annual attrition rate of a practice with no sale involved and is often as low as 2%. In fact, the average transition experience of buyers is over 10% growth in production six months after a sale. The bottom line is that typically the transfer of dental practices is highly successful for both sellers and buyers.

The overall concept in the transfer of patients is the transfer of trust. The dentist these patients have trusted for years is now recommending that his or her patients meet and give the new dentist buying the practice an opportunity to be their new dentist. Patients think:

"The dentist I have been seeing for years is retiring. I am going to have to go to a new dentist one way or the other. I can go to the dentist recommended by my dentist, the dentist I have trusted for years, or I can start shopping around for a totally new, unfamiliar dentist. I can go to a new practice where I don't know anybody, or I can try the new dentist at the practice I have been going to where I've known the receptionist and dental assistant for years, and where the hygienist knows me and my individual dental concerns and needs. The staff knows me and my family, and the practice is in a location that is convenient for me."

It just makes sense that the vast majority of patients will at least give the new dentist a try. It is then the responsibility of the new dentist to make a good first impression and win over the patients.

There are some circumstances a buyer should be aware of that can imperil the success of an effective patient transfer in a newly purchased practice. The first involves practices that have recently been relocated. Take the situation of a practice that was moved by the seller from an urban location to the suburbs within three years of the practice sale. When the selling dentist moved the practice, the vast majority of patients stayed with it; however, now that it is being sold to a new dentist so the selling dentist can retire, many of the patients may take this opportunity to find a dentist in a more convenient location. Another example is one in which a selling dentist originally lived close to his practice, but then moved his residence some distance away. Over the years, many of his friends and social acquaintances from the area of his residence drove well out of their way to see him for their dental care. The risk here again is that when this dentist retires, these patients may decide to find a dentist closer to home. For these reasons, it is important for practice buyers, as part of their pre-purchase due diligence, to check the zip codes of the patients of the practice. Do this through a chart audit prior to the sale to see where the majority of the patients-of-record live and work. The patients who are coming from zip codes that are a considerable distance from the practice may not stay with it after the sale.

One last important bit of advice to buyers regarding the retention of patients through the transition is to avoid, as best you can, making any significant changes to the practice for at least the first six to 12 months after the purchase. That is, do not make any changes to the basic operation of the practice, such as staff members, office hours, and financial and dental insurance office policies.

CHAPTER 8

Winning in Financing

Now that you have decided to own your own practice, how will you pay for it? Few dentists — either new grads or those who have been practicing for some time — have enough spare cash to fully fund the purchase of an existing practice or the equipment and building needed to start their own practice. Most prospective owners will have to finance most, if not all, of the cost or their practice acquisition or startup. Obtaining the right financing can make the difference between a prospering practice and one that just barely makes it.

When approaching the subject of financing, it helps to think that you are essentially purchasing money. The interest rate is the price tag on your loan — and with such a large investment it is crucial to secure the best rate possible for yourself. To win in financing, it is crucial to become educated about the process. Understanding a lender's point of view, and learning what you can do to secure the best interest rate possible, can ultimately save you thousands of dollars.

Still, there is much more to a loan than an interest rate. You will want to find a lender who really understands the dental industry and will work to help you succeed. It is also important to secure loan terms that are best for your specific situation. For instance, you might want to make larger monthly payments over a shorter repayment period, or smaller monthly payments over a longer period of time. And if you might want to refinance in a few years, you will want to be very careful not to accept a loan with a large pre-payment penalty.

The bottom line is that the more educated you are about the basic subject, the better you position yourself to win in financing.

First: Your Credit Rating

Never has money been more available to dentists at reasonable terms and interest rates than during the past few years. Yet, it is nearly impossible for a person who has bad credit to get a loan.

Unfortunately, this is a comment some dentists hear from lending institutions when attempting to secure a loan for a practice transition: "I'm sorry, but we are not comfortable making the loan due to your poor credit history."

What constitutes bad credit?

- *Bankruptcy*
- *Slow Pay*
These are payments made after the due date of the payment — usually 30 days or more. Often a payment coupon will have a "late after" or "late charge after" on the statement. This is not the due date! If late charges or reminder notices are sent on a regular basis, a report to the credit bureau will most likely show delinquency in payment.

- *Maxed-Out Credit*
If, for example, a borrower has five credit cards, each with a $5,000 line of credit, and four of them are at the maximum and the fifth has $4,500 charged against it, a lender presumes that

the borrower is living off these credit cards, or certainly spending beyond his or her means.

So what can be done? When a dentist has filed for bankruptcy in the past, there are many lenders who will not approve a loan under any circumstances, and some will lend only if the bankruptcy was over 10 years ago. Regarding slow pay or maxed-out credit issues, a simple explanation can go a long way toward getting the lending process back on track. Lenders want to make loans and recognize that there is often a logical explanation behind what otherwise looks to be a ding to the dentist's credit. Consider two examples:

- Late pays on student loans. It is very common for the wires to get crossed when a dentist applies for and is granted deferment on student loan debt. The result is that the loans are inadvertently reported as having been past due for 30 to 60 days all at the same time, and the dentist's credit score takes a nose dive. This is an easy situation to explain and show evidence of (e.g., all of the loans being past due at the same time and for the same period of time).

- A dentist lived off of his credit cards after moving to Florida and while he was looking for a job. This resulted in an increased exposure to credit card debt, the maxing out of his available credit, and the subsequent reduction of his credit score. By explaining all of this to the lender, this dentist was able to secure approval for his financing needs as the lender found comfort in the combination of the dentist's explanation, a review of his credit report, and the relative absence of any abuse of credit prior to the move.

A factor that is less likely to be deemed evidence of bad credit, but that can negatively impact a dentist's credit score is "loan shopping." Loan shopping is the process of applying to different institutions for the same loan. When someone applies for a loan, the first thing the lending institution does is run a credit check. Every time a credit check is done, it shows up on the applicant's credit report and will remain there for up to two years. Excessive credit checks will decrease a person's personal credit score.

Establishing and maintaining good credit is not difficult; it just takes a conscious effort and the knowledge of how a personal credit rating is determined.

Selecting a Lender

Choosing the right lender to work with is no easy task, whether you are just starting out in practice or have been in business for a while. There are literally hundreds of lenders to choose from, and each offers basically the same products and services. So how do you choose the right one?

Begin by being skeptical of the gimmicks and giveaways intended to draw dentists in. These lures usually represent a transactional relationship characterized by a "one-size-fits-all" mentality that in no way guarantees your ongoing financing needs will be met.

The real value, and the real difference, is in the relationship. For example, some lenders might have you deal with a different person every time you need assistance, while another might have you do business with one person who understands your total financial picture and has both the authority and capabilities to handle your needs. The latter is often referred to as "relationship lending," because the focus is on establishing a healthy and long-term relationship between you, the borrower and the banker that is designed to address your specific financial needs.

Planning the Approach

Before selecting a lender, you should decide exactly what you are seeking. The following are desirable "relationship" characteristics to look for:

- A history of lending to service businesses. There is a world of difference between a lender who is experienced in lending on the cash flow of a service business and one whose primary experience is in lending on the value of inventory, supplies, receivables, real estate, etc.

• A true understanding of the business of dentistry, and a special interest in and willingness to deal with dentists as highly skilled trade professionals

• A certain amount of money (e.g., a dentist in need of $600,000 to purchase a practice will find an offer of $500,000 from a lender with a great interest rate of no use)

• Reasonable rates and financing terms

The next step is to marshal a strong case for why you deserve financial backing, both as a prospective or existing business owner and as a trained and licensed dental professional. If, for example, you are looking for a $150,000 loan with a six-year term, you must be able to present clearly defined reasons why those particular needs should be met. It may sound simplistic, but all too often borrowers approach lenders with no real argument in support of their financing needs.

The Initial Meeting

The initial meeting with the lender of choice is the most critical stage of the process. At that meeting, you should provide the following information in support of your stated financial needs:

• Historical statements of year-end assets, liabilities and income (for existing practice owners, the last three annual tax returns will often suffice, and for those acquiring practices, the last three annual tax returns of the seller will do)

• Information regarding the "discretionary expenses" of the practice (defined as expenses including owner's compensation, which are either not geared to or have nothing at all to do with the production of dental receipts — examples include profit-sharing, auto lease payments, travel and entertainment, office rent, owner's salary, charitable contributions, interest expense, etc.)

- A comprehensive depiction of the practice's historical financial performance, from the perspective of operating income before discretionary expenses

- Evidence of the practice's most recent accounts receivable aging total (this information is important to include because many lenders prefer accounts receivable as collateral)

- A written description of the current physical characteristics of the practice (locations, number of employees, number of operators, active patient count, revenue payer mix, room for expansion, unique services provided, physical plant, staff, terms of office lease, etc.)

- A comprehensive vision of the practice's future, noting any changes to the services offered, physical plant, staff, etc.

- An illustration of the practice acquisition transition strategy to be employed. For example, this might involve the listing of services performed and hours worked by the seller versus the expanded services and hours of the buyer, anticipated post-acquisition activities by the seller focused on introducing the buyer to the staff and patients of the practice, anticipated clinical work to be performed by the seller including compensation and other terms of the seller's employment, etc.

- A furniture and equipment value estimate

To set the stage for a highly productive initial meeting, you should think of the lender as a partner with whom you are about to enter into the practice of dentistry. More often than not, you will be responsible for setting the initial pace for the meeting with the lender. This is best done by providing information on the practice and making clear your desired loan amount, pricing and terms.

Gauging Lender Reaction

Once you have organized all of the pertinent practice information of interest to the lender and have clearly communicated it at the initial meeting, be prepared to observe the lender's reaction to your presentation. The desired lender will be one who shows a sincere interest in the facts and materials provided; who sees the wisdom in providing financing in support of an income stream; who is interested in establishing a long-term relationship based on financing successful business opportunities; and who is likely to provide the amount of money you need at reasonable pricing and terms. Lenders who appear to be overly focused on the value of the practice's equipment and accounts receivable, the equity in your home, or whether you have a solid co-maker/guarantor candidate typically are transaction-oriented rather than relationship-oriented. Transaction-oriented lenders often charge higher rates, take excessive collateral, and provide less money than is needed.

Be sure to respond to the lender's questions, concerns and recommendations. You should respect the lender's comments and questions, as they may cover areas you have overlooked due to emotional attachments or status as a long-time owner. A lender's analytical perspective may be deemed a breath of fresh air or out of left field, but in comparison to other advisors, a lender's charge for advice is cheap.

Communication Is Key

Lenders who cater to dental practices and their owners recognize the significant value of a dental business as a relatively reliable stream of cash flow. They also recognize that for such relationships to be mutually beneficial, the above-mentioned quantitative (historical and projected numbers) and qualitative (story behind the numbers) analysis of the dental practice must be readily available and clearly communicated at the initial meeting.

As the borrower, you should remember that you are in control of the loan negotiation process. Lenders are in the business of selling money and other financial services. They are looking for a reason to give dentists money. Do not leave it to the lender to think of all the right questions to ask or all the right information to seek. A lender will never know a dentist's business as well as the dentist does. Without a clear understanding of the business, or confidence in the individual borrower's ability to efficiently operate the business, most lenders will be willing to provide financing only at a percentage of hard collateral value (i.e., transactional lending resulting in a loan of $150,000 or less).

There can be no secrets between you and your lender. The key to a successful relationship is communication. Then and only then will the lender understand where you are coming from, and be able to formulate solutions designed to accommodate your specific financial needs.

Who Does a Banker See When Looking at a Young Dentist?

Sometimes there seems to be a disconnect from the very start between a prospective lender and a young dentist eager to set up his or her own practice. Take this example:

A young dentist is sitting across from a loan officer at a bank. The loan officer is looking through the two-inch-thick stack of papers representing the dentist's application for a loan to buy his first dental practice. The dentist knows the practice is a winner and that all the documents are in order. So why is there a little frown on the loan officer's face when she looks at the dentist?

Perhaps it's because most bankers see themselves when they meet a dentist or any other prospective borrower for the first time. This tendency has been at work for as long as there have been banks and banking officers, and the implications are generally negative for young dentists if left unchecked. The reason for this tendency is rooted in the differences between a dentist and the average BBA/MBA banker early in their respective careers.

Most newly minted business school grads enter the workaday world with book knowledge of the tools they will need to conduct business but little, if any, experience in using the tools in a productive manner. Therefore, they are generally ill-equipped to make money for anyone straight out of school. On the other hand, most dentists graduate with a clear knowledge of the tools in their tool boxes; furthermore, they have experience using the tools to provide a valuable service that the marketplace will gladly purchase. In other words, a recent dental graduate is a highly skilled professional able to earn a good living at the same time that a young banker resembles a relative "lump of clay" still needing a lot of molding. As might be expected, this difference can be a real stumbling block when the typical young dentist (two or three years out of school) meets the typical banker with a financing request. The banker is apt to see not a qualified borrower sitting across the table, but himself or herself at that stage in his or her career. The solution to this problem is simple: Know your opponent, be prepared to persuasively argue your case and, if possible, choose a more experienced lender.

Be Prepared with Solid Arguments

Young dentists should prepare their arguments in advance to help their banker understand that they are superbly prepared to earn a good living and repay the practice loan. In addition to having all the information on the practice to be purchased or started up, they should point out to the banker:

- The level and breadth of skill and knowledge required to pass the dental boards

- The value of a dental degree in terms of the limited number of dentists graduating each year and the tremendously favorable ratio of dentists relative to the population of the United States in general and in the community in which the dentist plans to practice dentistry in particular

- The value of a dental degree in terms of the increased earning power of a dentist relative to the national median income in the United States; by the way, this increased power works out right now to a present value in excess of $1 million, which more than offsets the cost/debt incurred in pursuit of the degree

The bottom line is that if a young dentist invests time in making sure the banker gains the proper understanding of who he or she is and the value of a trade in dentistry, the request for financing will be positioned in the proper light and thus have a far greater opportunity for success.

Choose a More Experienced Lender

Small business bankers generally receive a great deal less commercial credit training than their middle market and large corporate banker peers. As a result, they tend to operate and lean heavily on strict lending guidelines (such as, advance 60% against inventory, 50% against accounts receivable, 30% against equipment). Therefore, when they find themselves with an opportunity to advance funds against the present value of a dentist's future earning capacity, they experience a natural conflict between the lending opportunity at hand and their formula mindset.

One solution to this problem is to take a lot of time with the small business banker, and perhaps involve your accountant or some other third-party financial consultant, to fully educate him or her about the business of dentistry and the value inherent in a dental practice. A more efficient solution is to bypass the small business banker altogether and go directly to the bank president or one of the more experienced middle market corporate bankers. Banking professionals at this level typically have the expertise to understand and evaluate a dental practice financing opportunity, and they have the clout to deliver a speedy yes or no on a loan request. Of course, it would be wise for young dentists to give even bankers at this level the opportunity to adjust their perspective to accommodate the tremendous value of a dental degree.

Another solution is to go to a lending institution focused on understanding dentists and their businesses. Fortunately, because traditional bank financiers so often just don't get it, two types of lenders specialized in providing financing to dentists have emerged.

- The first are lenders that utilize their experience and expertise to assist dentists and conventional bank financiers in realizing a meeting of the minds. They help dentists understand the informational needs of the bank, and prepare their financing requests to communicate their needs in a form the banker will understand and find compelling. They further assist both the dentist and banker through the often complex loan closing process.

• The second are lenders that directly fund hundreds of millions of dollars in financing to dentists every year in a speedy and efficient manner. Their approach to the dental market is grounded in the law of large numbers. In other words, they understand that history and experience have shown dentists to be second only to veterinarians as the highest quality small business borrowers. Therefore, they relax the level of their investigation of individual lending opportunities in favor of delivering speedy approvals and quick closings (qualities in a financing transaction which are highly prized by many dentists). They do this assuming that, no matter how carefully they evaluate any given lending opportunity, only one out of every 100 loans made to dentists will result in a loss, and if interest rates are set high enough, the money made on the good loans will justify the periodic bad loan. As noted, loans from these specialized lenders typically feature a higher interest rate and other terms and conditions designed to compensate them for the risks that their speedy approach leaves uncovered.

Reviewing a Financing Offer

Once a lender makes you a financing offer, review it very, very carefully — including the fine print. You will want to look for two things in particular:

• *Annual Percentage Rate (APR)*
The APR is a measure of the total costs of the financing offer. Such costs include the interest rate paid over the life of the loan, any fees paid, and any interest to be paid on interest as a result of having no payments or graduated payments during the first few months of the loan.

• *Penalties for Early Repayment*

Some lenders will charge a penalty if the loan is repaid during the first few years of the loan or at any time prior to the scheduled maturity of the loan. It is not unusual for penalties of $30,000 to $40,000 to be levied on loans as small as $150,000.

LIBOR Rate, Prime Rate, 10-Year U.S. Treasury Rate, Federal Funds Rate – What Does It All Mean?

Many dentists have called their bankers over the years to ask about refinancing their fixed-rate business loans after hearing reports of decreases in the "prime rate" and/or observing low home loan rates. In most instances, they were subsequently disappointed to find that business loan rates had not decreased in step with reductions in the prime rate and were a good bit higher than the rates available for residential mortgage loans. Why?

Home Loan Rates vs. Commercial/Business Loan Rates

Rates for home loans are lower than rates for commercial/business loans because home loans are considered to represent considerably

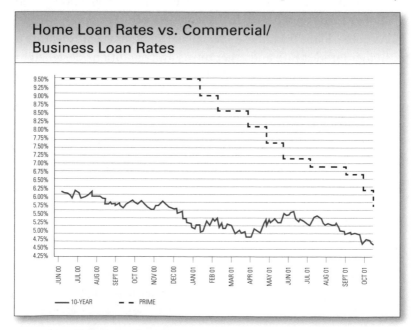

less risk to lenders than loans secured by the equipment, patient records, goodwill and/or receivables of a dental practice. For lenders, accepting increased risk requires that they receive an increased rate of return (i.e., a higher interest rate) relative to other less risky loans and/or investments that the bank's cash could be put into. Therefore, although home loan rates and fixed-rate commercial loans may move up or down in a relatively complementary manner, a fixed-rate loan to a dentist to purchase a dental practice will typically be at least 2% to 2.5% higher than the average 30-year fixed-rate home loan.

Short-Term vs. Long-Term Rates

Rate activity in 2000 and 2001 was revealing in regard to the movement of long-term rates versus short-term rates. In 2001, lenders, existing borrowers, prospective borrowers and investors witnessed historic activity in the movement of short-term financing rates (depicted in the chart comparing the 10-year treasury and prime rate movement in 2000 and 2001), as in just nine months the Federal Reserve discount rate and prime rate decreased from 9.5% and 6% to 2% and 5.5% respectively (an unprecedented size and

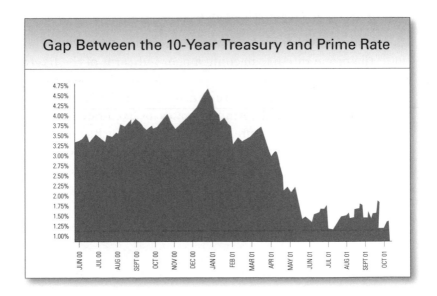

Gap Between the 10-Year Treasury and Prime Rate

rate of decline to lows not seen since the Kennedy administration in the early 1960s). This decline in short-term rates:

• Was the product of the U.S. government's response to the perceived threat to the health of the U.S. economy represented by the bursting of the dot-com bubble and the sundry problems following in the wake of that troubling event, and,

• Was not matched by similar movement in fixed rates set by investor demand for U.S. Treasury notes and bonds (the free market rates illustrated herein by the 10-year Treasury note rate).

Free market long-term fixed rates had anticipated the need for reduced rates in advance of the actions of the Federal Reserve. Free market forces reduced the 10-year Treasury note rate from 6.25% to 5% during the second half of 2000. In fact, by January 2001, just before the Federal Reserve finally began to reduce short-term rates, the gap between the prime rate (held steady by the Federal Reserve at 9.5% during most of 2000) and the 10-year U.S. Treasury note rate reached a historic high of 4.5% (see the peak of the chart to the right). As a consequence, by late 2000, the interest rate for a floating rate business loan (9.5%) was higher than would be set for a five- to 10-year fixed-rate business loan (8.5%).

As was so clearly depicted in the movement of rates in 2000 and 2001, the prime rate has become a poor indicator of the likely movements in interest rates charged on fixed-rate business loans. The 10-year Treasury note rate is generally accepted today as the benchmark rate for determining rates for fixed-rate business loans. As a result, dentists interested in getting a quick sense of the business financing rates they are likely to be offered can do so by adding 3.5% to the 10-year Treasury note rate quoted in the news.

CHAPTER 9

The Numbers Count

Roughly 110,000 dentists' offices and clinics operate in the U.S., generating annual revenues of $40 billion, according to the U.S. Census Bureau. The vast majority of dentists are sole practitioners. Of the approximately 150,000 dentists, 80% practice general dentistry, while the rest specialize in orthodontics, oral surgery, periodontics, endodontics, pedodontics and prosthodontics. The average annual revenue per office is about $600,000, and average personal income for dentists is $175,000.

The average practice has 4,000 patient visits a year, with an average charge of $125 per visit. Because of the relatively small charge per visit, and because even a big dental bill is small compared to big medical bills, insurance penetration and the issue of cost-containment have been much lower in dentistry than in medicine. Nationally, more than 140 million people have dental benefit plans. Traditional fee-for-service remains the most popular dental option among employees nationally, while dental HMOs and PPOs are in second and third place, respectively.

The typical dentist office includes dental hygienists and assistants, and office staff. The average office has one dentist and three other employees, a receptionist, a chairside assistant and a hygienist. Insurance paperwork, bill collection, scheduling and ordering supplies are the main concerns of the office staff.

Many dentists claim that they don't have time to apply sufficient attention to business matters such as overhead expenses, supplies and a marketing plan. Others just admit that they have a hard time getting motivated to give business matters the attention needed. The fact remains they should do everything in their power to make time to maintain the business side of the practice. For a dentist to ignore the business side of his or her practice is to set in motion a process that results in the dentist working harder and harder for less and less money as the overhead creeps up and profit margins shrink.

Every day, dentists all over the country will call their accountants or other advisors and say, "I feel I'm not doing well." When these same dentists are subsequently asked about the status of their practice's production, collections, overhead, new patient visits, total patient visits and recall activity, the response most often given is, "I don't know." Not knowing the numbers leads to feelings of helplessness and frustration. It will ultimately result in dental practice owners making uninformed decisions based on subjective judgment.

Taking X-rays of a patient's mouth in order to carefully identify problems and craft the most effective clinical treatment plan is fundamental to the practice of clinical dentistry. No less should be done in the identification and development of the most effective means of solving business problems. Sometimes after taking an X-ray of a patient's mouth the counsel offered the patient is, "We will wait until your next visit, and check for any change that might necessitate action." The same is often true for business problems.

Whether a clinical or business situation, diagnosing the problem and planning possible future courses of action is in and of itself a comforting exercise. The equivalent diagnostic tool of an X-ray in the business setting is the practice's numbers. A good handle on the numbers and what they indicate as to the health and opportunities of a practice allow one to take the most effective business steps in matters of staffing, facility enlargement, moving the practice or adding an associate.

Some dentists feel that business statistics and numbers are incompatible with a service orientation toward patients, but just the opposite is true. Data is vital in assisting dentists in achieving their visions and goals for their practices. For example, if the 25 new patients per month do not share the dentist's philosophy of care, then this number doesn't reflect progress toward the dentist's goals. However, the number of new patients fitting the profile the dentist has targeted would be helpful to know.

Dental Practice Fees

Dr. Charles Blair's nationally acclaimed Revenue Enhancement Program offers fee analysis and related procedure mix consulting. Dentists participating in his program have realized an average increase in practice profitability of over $80,000 annually. Having reviewed over 3,500 practices, Dr. Blair notes that most doctors have no idea where their fee schedule stands in relation to other dentists in their local area. His experience shows that most dentists operate with a schizophrenic fee schedule, with some fees below the 50th percentile (managed care), some fees above the 95th percentile, and the remaining fees all across the board. Using zip code specific fee data for each participating practice, Dr. Blair provides an analysis setting forth the fees for each ADA code at the 50th, 75th, 85th, 90th, and 95th percentiles for that doctor's zip code.

Dental Practice Fees

- Average practice fee schedule is 5% to 15% below the reimbursement levels allowed by institutional payors
- Fee increases can produce the single largest immediate impact on a practice's net

According to Dr. Blair, the first step doctors should take to improve profitability is to simply set their fees in a rational manner. He recommends that doctors select a fee percentile appropriate to their practice and the quality of care they are providing. Once selected, all fees below that percentile should be moved immediately to that specific percentile. Any fees that are already above the selected fee percentile would remain at their current level. This results in a fee schedule that is more fair to the doctor, patient and insurance company alike, and has produced dramatic results for Dr. Blair's clients.

Average Dentist Sets Fees by:

- The standard that was in place when the practice was purchased
- Advice from other dentists
- Periodically reading magazine surveys

The Root of the Matter

Two common mistakes unnecessarily depress dentists' incomes and therefore, their ability to keep their practices up to date.

The Root of the Matter

- Average practice would realize a level net profit result, despite the loss of 300 active patients, with a 10% increase in the average fee schedule

The first is that most dentists undercharge their patients and relatively few overcharge. There are many reasons for charging below fair value, but regardless of the reason, a dentist who charges below the fair value will work harder, make less each year and retire with a smaller retirement income.

The second mistake is that too many dentists fail to raise their fees incrementally on a regular basis. These dentists go years without increases and then impose large, catch-up fee increases all at once. Large, erratic fee increases cause anxiety for the dentist, increase patient complaints and prevent the dentist from earning a stable yet increasing rate of personal compensation. No dentist benefits from such easily avoidable mistakes.

Negotiating Fees with Patients

Patient: "Doctor, your fees for this treatment plan seem awfully high to me. I called the dentist down the block and he could do it for a lot less."

You have invested years of education and financial sacrifice to master your craft. Yet, invariably, you continue to encounter patients who question your right to be adequately compensated. In addition, the patient is making you feel that you are overpriced for the marketplace and can't compete. You worry about losing the time you've invested in preparing the treatment plan if the patient goes to another practice that is cutting fees to compete. While all of these thoughts and emotions may come to mind, more than likely, the reality of the situation is that the patient is setting the stage to negotiate.

Though the patient is saying that in his opinion, "Your fees for this treatment plan seem awfully high," the fact of the matter is that the patient usually doesn't have the slightest clue what it costs you to provide the treatment. In fact, most dentists don't know what it costs to deliver the dental care they provide. Therefore, the call to the dentists "down the block" (if it was done at all) was the patient's way of paving the way for the negotiation of a lower fee. In response, you have several choices:

- Cave and cut your fee
- Act offended and run the patient off
- Play the game

Choice one, cutting your fee, communicates that your clinical skill is overpriced and your fees are negotiable. On top of this, you're conceding that the patient and the "doctor down the block" have a better handle on the value of your clinical skill and service than you do.

In choice number two, everyone loses. You get upset and lose a patient. The patient may receive inferior treatment from the "doctor down the block." Finally, the "doctor down the block" loses more and more professional credibility and income while thinking he is winning the game.

Choice number three, playing the game, means understanding that you and the patient are really negotiating on the quality of the patient's health care. In any game of negotiation, real success is measured by the degree to which both players feel that they have won. So with this in mind, let's look at the most effective reply to our patient's comment:

> *Patient: "Doctor, your fees for this treatment plan seem awfully high to me. I called the doctor down the block and he said he could do it for a lot less."*

> *Dentist: "Mr. Makeadeal, our fees accurately reflect the quality of our service."*

Nothing more needs to be said at this point. You have successfully assisted the prospective patient in making a connection between the value of your expertise and the fee you charge for delivering care. The implication to the patient is that if they want their treatment performed with lesser quality materials or by a less experienced dentist, they are free to go elsewhere without any feelings of shame or embarrassment. Most patients will stop negotiating at this point and accept treatment with a feeling of comfort that the fee they will pay is in line with the value they receive (a win-win).

A few patients will persist in arguing. Usually, those who persist in complaining about the level of your fees are not the kind of patients you want in your practice. These patients do not value you as a uniquely skilled dental professional. If and when, despite your offers of a full range of payment alternatives to make the treatment plan affordable, Mr. Makeadeal leaves to pursue the deal offered by the "doctor down the block," you can forward his X-rays, confident in your position (a win-win).

The last, but very important step to be taken in this "negotiation game" is for you to state that, "If for any reason you would like to return to our practice, please don't hesitate to call us. We'll be glad to have you back." This is important because a customer who perceives he has been "told off" and thus has had a bad experience is much more likely to talk about it than one who recalls his last encounter with you as one conducted in an environment of mutual respect and dignity.

In these types of encounters the key word is "confidence." The level of your fees should be set at a level you truly feel confident in charging. If you feel that your fees are representative of the quality of the materials you use as well as your experience in performing the treatment, your patients will perceive that you know your worth as a highly skilled dental professional.

How Much Should Fees Be Raised?

The unique thing about raising fees is the resulting increase in collections flows straight to bottom-line profits. In contrast, all other strategies for increasing profits, though they may be necessary and effective, are initiated with an increase in practice overhead (increased costs for staff, marketing, collections, consulting fees, etc.). Thus, whatever good arises from these efforts must first cover the added cost of bringing on favorable results.

In understanding the need for, and the amount by which fees should be adjusted upward, most dentists would do well to first take the time to understand inflation and its effect on their practice. It is important to remember that inflation acts as a hidden tax on your income. Therefore, if the cost of your services goes up by 5% and you raise your fees only 3%, the 2% difference comes out of your pocket. A simple method for measuring the impact of inflation on your practice is to take the estimated consumer inflation rate of 3% and divide it by 12 to get a monthly inflation factor (.03/12=.0025). This can then be multiplied by the number of months since your last fee increase to get the increase in consumer inflation since then (eight months would mean .0025x8 or 2%). Because ADA reports indicate the inflationary pressure on the operating costs of dental practices is higher than that represented in consumer inflation rate, the results of the above exercise represents the low end of the deteriorative effect of inflation on your practice.

While raising fees to stay in step with the cost of inflation within your practice will prevent a gradual deterioration in profitability, you must remember that when it comes to the base cost of dental care delivery, not all practices are alike. Some dentists utilize more costly supplies, lab services and/or equipment in their effort to deliver their unique mix of dental care. This means that one size does not fit all when it comes to setting fees. Remember that quality treatment must be supported by fees. The fees you charge should adequately compensate you while allowing you to maintain your staff, facilities and continuing education at the highest levels.

Fees and Practice Value in Transitions

Despite the obviously positive implications for practice profitability and value, many dentists are reluctant to raise fees in the years leading up to the sale of their practice. Most of these prospective sellers are winding down their careers, and thus believe themselves to be financially sound, and are reluctant to "burden" their patients with fee increases. However, a dentist who has not raised fees for 36 months passes on a need for a 9% fee increase if the buyer is to make up ground lost to inflation alone.

"Who cares what the former owner did or didn't do with the fee levels of the practice. The buyer can fix that problem!" Unfortunately, it's not that simple. Even in instances where buyers increase fees as a necessary act to cover ground lost by the seller to inflation, the mere act of increasing fees is often viewed by the patients and staff of the practice as a negative act rather than the appropriate adjustment to market. As a result, buyers will rarely purchase a practice with fee increases as a key element of their transition plan. Rather, they will make a discounted offer for the practice such that the fee structure in place is justified, by the price paid for the practice. In other words, dentists who have been reluctant to keep the level of their fees in line with the quality and method of their approach to dental care delivery, and in line with inflationary increases, end up paying for this lack of vigilance twice — once in the reduced practice income while they operated it, and the second time in the form of the reduced price for which the practice is sold.

Dental practices netting 40% or more before compensation for professional dental services are in highest demand. These practices are most likely to ensure compensation of 28% to 30% for the doctor and leave 13% to 15% for debt service and capital improvements. Very often practices put up for sale net less than 40% because their fees are below market for their area. Most buyers are not interested in purchasing a seller's problems. Therefore, sellers need to correct overstaffing, as well as staff compensation and fee schedule problems before the practice is sold. The alternative, as previously noted, is for sellers to accept significantly discounted values for their practices.

Some sellers think that patients will leave if fees are increased. In fact, less than 10% of patients will even notice a fee increase from $650 to $710. The same fee increase made by the seller will result in less than 1% of the patients making an issue of the increase, while the same very reasonable and appropriate change made by the buyer typically creates a real sense of outrage and confusion for a majority of both the staff and patients of the practice.

Treatment Acceptance

Most practices are losing a huge amount of income because they do not have a smooth system in place to help the patient overcome the barriers to treatment acceptance. Second to fee increases, there is no faster way to improve collections, production, and the bottom line than improving a practice's treatment acceptance. Dr. Charles Blair's nationally acclaimed Profits Plus+ Workshop computes over 100 different statistics for each participating doctor's dental practice and provides industry benchmarks for comparison purposes. One ratio he measures is called the Conversion Rate. This ratio measures the doctor's ability to persuade patients to accept treatment when it is recommended. This ratio is simply the actual production divided by the total production recommended. Dr. Blair notes that in general dentistry, pedodontics, and endodontics, the conversion rate averages over 90%. In other specialties such as periodontics, oral surgery and orthodontics, the average conversion rate is lower, with orthodontics having the lowest rate of around 70%.

A key component in improving and maintaining a strong Conversion Rate is using a treatment coordinator. The treatment coordinator's job is to speak to the patient in private to help them overcome the barriers that may interfere with their willingness to proceed with treatment. The treatment coordinator is able to discuss the treatment plan and the available payment options. It is with the treatment coordinator that the patient can voice their concerns and overcome their fears. If the barrier to treatment is purely financial concerns, the treatment coordinator will work with the patient and direct them to several external financial institutions that help patients finance treatment. If the patient has a clinical concern, the treatment coordinator can involve the dentist for further explanation.

Typically, in all major expense decisions (such as buying a house or car) the opinions of the decision makers in the family are necessary. Therefore, any dentist and/or treatment coordinator who presents a treatment plan to a patient, but not to their spouse, runs the risk that the message gets lost or watered down in translation, and the spouse says, "Honey, you don't need veneers. Your teeth are fine." If, on the other hand, care is taken to involve the decision maker, they are far more likely to understand and appreciate the need for the treatment as well as the potential benefit to the patient.

Billing

As in the delivery of clinical dental care or the implementation of any other activity where the effective application of technique and skill can improve outcome, billing is an area where a savvy approach to a seemingly mundane chore can yield surprising results. Several important recommendations for the creation of a billing statement most likely to encourage prompt payment are:

- Each billing statement should have a due date by which patients are expected to submit payment. Every other bill they receive has a required payment date and consequences if a timely payment is not made. A common payment deadline is 10 days or two weeks from the statement date.

- The billing statement should be formatted to allow patients to choose to pay by credit card by writing in a credit card number.

- Each statement should include a payment envelope that is addressed to the office, so as to require as little effort as possible on the part of the paying patient.

- Customize the message on the statement. Patients respond to messages that are directed at them personally. For example, "We did not receive our payment on July 15th as requested. If you are experiencing financial difficulty, please contact our office. Otherwise, we would appreciate payment in full no later than August 6." No one likes to see themselves as having financial difficulty.

- If not daily, bills should be sent out at least weekly. Don't wait to send bills once a month.

- The financial coordinator should be able to determine the amount anticipated from the insurance company.

- When it comes to handling insurance, file claims electronically and immediately. Electronic claims submission significantly improves payment turnaround time.

Collections

When a patient is scheduled for treatment, a set amount of time is blocked out for that patient. At the time of service, the practice incurs all the labor and overhead costs associated with treatment delivery. When the fees for the procedure go uncollected, the revenue for that procedure is lost, the costs of providing the service is sunk, and the opportunity to have delivered dental services to a paying patient slips by.

Most practices report a collections ratio (total collections divided by total production) of 96-98%. However, a surprising number of dentists have a collection ratio below this level.

Fundamental to the increase and maintenance of a solid collections ratio is a clear and consistent written financial policy and procedures, which should include the following key steps:

1. Educate Patients

Make information available that educates patients on the benefits insurance can provide for particular treatments. Staff should be trained to be knowledgeable about these benefits so patients have a clear picture of what portion of a fee is covered by insurance and what is not.

2. Clarify Accountability in Advance

Make sure patients are aware of the fees they will be responsible for prior to treatment. This prevents any misunderstandings and allows any necessary payment schedule to be worked out in advance.

3. Provide Access to Third-Party Financing

Offer third-party patient financing through an external finance company. Such a company can often pre-approve patients for financing before the treatment even begins. This allows the practice to be reimbursed immediately for the treatment performed.

Many dental practice owners are nipping the collections problem in the bud on the front end of the process through the addition of a dedicated financial coordinator to the practice team. A well-trained financial coordinator is prepared to:

- Politely and diplomatically educate the patient about what the practice can't do and, more importantly, what it can and will do to help the patient proceed with necessary/desired treatment

- Ensure that patients are versed on financial options well before treatment is scheduled

- Collect at the time of service and request payment in full for procedures that are under, for example, $250

- Clearly explain the office's payment options for more expensive procedures, including:

  - *Offering a slight adjustment in the fees, (such as 5%, for higher dollar procedures paid in full)*

  - *Partnering with a patient financing company (such as CareCredit) in lieu of allowing patients to carry balances on their accounts*

- Explain the advantages of treatment financing to patients, as well as, answer any questions

Accounts Receivable

Ninety-five percent of a practice's patient base should pay all fees due within 60 days of service, because the odds of collecting on accounts due for more than 90 days are slim at best. A good goal is that 70% of the practice's patient receivables be no older than 30 days. Two steps to relieve collections problems are:

1. Credit Card Payments

Allowing patients to use credit cards for payment is a must in practices today. Very few patients have the ability to pay out-of-pocket for significant dental procedures, but credit cards allow them to pay in full up-front. Patients also have the option of preauthorizing automatic payments that are charged on a certain date every billing cycle. Again, this causes minimal overhead for the practice in terms of collections, and makes payment for dentistry more comfortable for patients.

2. *Phased Payments*

Some patients who cannot pay the total amount up-front will pay half of the treatment fee when treatment in initiated and half at the beginning of the patient's final treatment appointment, meaning there is no overhead required for billing or collections.

Doctor-Funded Credit

Many dentists believe they can save or make money by extending credit in-office. The fact is, while it works for some, it doesn't work for most.

In general, the cost of financing in-office is far more expensive than the fees charged by an out-of-office patient finance company because a large amount of practice staff time is spent sending statements and making collection calls each month. However, the biggest cost of an in-office financing program is the increase in broken appointments.

It is often said that "people who owe you money don't like you." Offices with in-house financing have an increased level of broken recall appointments. The resulting increase in overall broken appointment totals are two to three times that of practices using an outside patient finance company. Therefore, it is important to also note that "people who owe you money are more likely to break appointments and less likely to refer to you."

Productivity

Too often, a dentist will realize that "I'm not nearly as busy as I could be" and act to eliminate the perceived problem before conducting a careful evaluation of the situation to determine:

- whether the problem is real, and
- if so, whether it needs to be dealt with now or watched a little longer, and
- what the best solution is.

A dentist who sees a full line-up of patients from the beginning of the day to the end may feel successful because the practice cannot handle any more patients. However, a busy practice is not necessarily a profitable one. A practice is most effective when it is producing the maximum dentistry it can per each individual patient. A practice that sees 30 patients per day and averages only $150 of production per patient ($4,500) is not nearly as profitable as a practice that sees 20 patients a day, but averages $350 of production per patient ($7,000). This kind of daily difference ($2,500) can mean an additional $500,000 per year for a practice scheduling patients four days a week. The dramatic difference in revenue can be attributed to the fact that the "slower" practice has the time to present, sell and deliver more comprehensive dental care. The "slower" practice also will run more efficiently with less stress because the office manager has more time to focus on the most important tasks in the practice.

In an effort to fill the schedule and put "cheeks in chairs," many dentists pump up the marketing in pursuit of more new patients. The problem is that the time spent processing a new patient and the work typically done on new patients in no way equals what is initially spent in time and money to get them in the door. New patients will actually jam up the practice's front desk because they have questions to ask of the staff and vice versa. There is additional paperwork, including insurance and health histories, and new treatment plans that must be completed. Very often, a careful evaluation of the practice and its schedule would reveal that simply recalling existing patients for a continuance of their recommended care and/or increasing the sale of elective dentistry to existing patients would do the trick of "filling the schedule."

Three Steps to Increase Average Production Per Patient:

1. Oral Exam

Assure that a comprehensive oral health exam is scheduled for every patient, including periodontal probing, oral cancer brush biopsies, cosmetic dentistry evaluations, and potentially appropriate elective procedures. This will help dentists identify more dentistry that could benefit patients.

2. Scripts

Develop effective scripts for case presentation for the dentist, treatment coordinator and office manager. These scripts will focus patient attention on the benefits of recommended treatment.

3. Enhanced Chair Time

Offer patients the ability to have multiple procedures done in one appointment (when possible). Patients generally like having as much dentistry performed in a single visit as possible because it's more convenient.

Unfortunately, many dental teams take it for granted that patients are aware of the dental treatment opportunities available, and most patients assume the dentist and/or staff will tell them if there is a treatment they need to consider. The net result is no results. However, the implementation of the following simple steps can get the patient/practice relationship back on track, and greatly increase the per-patient productivity of a dental team and significantly increase practice profitability.

• Ask the patient how they feel about their smile. To not ask about their oral health goals is to deny the patient treatment opportunities.

• Ask several broad questions and listen to the responses. For example, "How well can you chew with your partial?" "How would you like it if your teeth were straight?" "Have you ever thought you would like to have a brighter smile?" "How do you feel about the spaces between your teeth?" and so on.

• Use the questions to better understand the value the patient places on oral health care and how they perceive their individual oral health condition.

• Encourage the patient to talk.

• If the dentist is not comfortable asking patients specifically how they feel about their smile, instruct the front desk team to help by handing patients a comparative smile brochure when they check in. This is an excellent and tremendously simple tool to get the patient thinking about their oral health and the appearance of their smile before the dentist ever utters a word.

• Educate the patient about treatments that are offered in the practice. Provide patients with professionally written and designed materials that educate them about services and procedures. Many of these are readily available through the American Dental Association.

Four Measures of Productivity Relative to Staff

Dr. Charles Blair's nationally acclaimed Profits Plus¹ Workshop monitors four key ratios in accessing the productivity of a practice relative to its staff:

• *Revenue Per Full-Time Employee*
This benchmark measures the practice's labor efficiency. It is determined by dividing the annual practice collections by the number of full-time staff, excluding lab employees and doctors. Dr. Blair has observed that most practices' annual revenue per full-time employee falls in the $125,000-$200,000 range, with an average of $160,000 per employee. Doctors below the industry benchmark may be suffering from any of the following: overstaffing, under-producing staff and/or doctor, or a low fee schedule.

• *Revenue Per Full-Time Business Employee*
If the prior benchmark indicates a labor problem, it's important to look closer at each of the three component areas (clerical,

chairside and hygiene). This ratio is determined by dividing the average monthly revenues for the past 12 months by the number of full-time employees in the clerical (front desk) area. Dr. Blair has observed that most practices are in the range of $40,000-$50,000 of revenue per month per full-time clerical employee, with an average of $45,000. Practices below the industry benchmark may be overstaffed in the business area, have underproductive employees, or inadequate revenues due to low fees or production, says Blair.

• *Monthly Revenues Per Chairside Employee*
This benchmark determines the labor efficiency of chairside employees and is calculated by dividing the monthly practice revenues by the number of full-time chairside employees. Dr. Blair has observed that the average revenues per full-time chairside fall in the range of $30,000 to $40,000 for most practices, with an average around $35,000. Below average practices may have overstaffing, low fees, poor production mix and/or inadequate doctor clinical speed.

• *Annual Revenue Per Full-Time Hygienist*
This ratio determines the overall productivity of the hygiene department and is calculated by dividing the annual hygiene revenue by the total number of full-time hygienists. Dr. Blair has observed that most practices fall within the range of $160,000 to $200,000 of revenue per full-time hygienist, with the average around $180,000. Below average production can result from poor scheduling, inadequate procedure mix, excessive broken appointments, or slow clinical speed.

The Dentist's Production
The critical factor in total office production is dentist production because it is the largest production source and has a dramatic impact on the performance of the practice. Dentist production principally originates from the following sources, which should be evaluated regularly and reviewed to ensure that each is contributing adequately:

• *Hygiene Patients*

A target of 75% plus of dentist production should come from hygiene patients. The hygienist often plays a major role in the identification of potential treatment areas. But this is calculated as dentist production because it is the dentist who treats the final case. Depending on the office, either the hygienist or dentist will present the treatment plan to the patient and initiate scheduling for the recommended procedures. Hygiene is the aortic valve of a dental practice, serving established and new patients. Whatever happens in those hygiene appointments has a great impact on the dentist's success.

• *New Patients*

A target of 20% of dentist production should come from new patients. Dentists should carefully evaluate the level of production that can be attributed to new patients. They also should track the "average production per new patient" both weekly and monthly. Remember, new patient examinations range from quick observations in a hygiene room to comprehensive examinations. The level of diagnostic and treatment identification will directly affect both the percentage of dentist production from new patients and total practice production.

• *Emergency Patients*

A target of no more than 10% of dentist production should come from emergency patients. Emergencies are an ongoing source of diagnostic and treatment services. The number of emergencies will be proportional to the level of care that has been provided and the number of active patients in the practice.

The Hygienist's Production

"The moment I take my hands out of my patient's mouth, my income stops." Almost every dentist comes to this realization at some point in his or her career. The solution involves the leveraging of the dentist's time and skill with the support of accredited staff. The reward is the addition of a stream of passive income to the dentist's earnings. In any business, passive income comes from the work of others. In a dental practice, passive income is principally realized through the labor of hygienists.

Dr. Charles Blair's nationally acclaimed Profits Plus+ Workshop computes over 100 different statistics for each participating doctor's dental practice and provides industry benchmarks for comparison purposes. Two benchmarks related to accessing the effectiveness of a dental practice's hygiene program are:

- *Adult Prophy to Perio Procedure Mix*
This statistic measures the percentage of total hygiene department production from adult prophys and perio-related procedures. Dr. Blair has observed that the average general practice reports a mix of 80% adult prophy revenue and 20% perio procedures from their hygiene department. A lower percentage of perio procedures usually indicates insufficient soft tissue management production due to lack of training, proper scheduling, coding errors, or inadequate diagnostic abilities.

- *Ratio of Hygiene Production to Total Compensation*
This is the most accurate measure of the hygienist's worth to the practice, and is calculated by dividing the total production of each hygienist (excluding doctor exam fees) by that hygienist's total compensation (includes salary, bonuses, payroll taxes and fringe benefits). While most practices desire a 3:1 ratio here, Dr. Blair has observed that the average ratio is around 2.5:1. The problem here can be either underproduction or overcompensation. This can be attacked on either front by revising the compensation formula to a percentage of total production, or increasing production through better scheduling, expanded hours, or increasing the mix of soft tissue management procedures.

Overhead

The importance of monitoring the practice's overhead or expenses cannot be stressed too strongly. Though most consultants and advisors to dentists agree that the ideal level for practice overhead is 55% of total receipts, it is important to note that every dental practice is different and it is common, and acceptable, for dental overhead to be as high as 60% to 65% of total receipts.

A dental practice has five major areas of expense:

1. Facility (rent/utilities)

2. Staff Salaries (employee taxes and benefits)

3. Dental Supplies

4. Laboratory

5. Miscellaneous (dues, subscriptions, legal bills, accountant fees, business taxes, telephone, marketing, goldfish food, office supplies, etc.)

As noted, the generally accepted ideal for overhead is 55% of practice collections for a general practitioner. Therefore, a dentist operating at 60% to 65% is either operating at an optimal level based on his or her unique clinical/business model or has room for some improvement, but in neither case needs to rush to slash costs. On the other hand, an office operating at a level of overhead exceeding 65% needs to quickly develop and execute a strategy for increasing production and/or reducing expenses. In order to identify areas of expense which may be robbing the dentist of net profit, baseline expense levels must be understood. The following are industry norm expense to collections percentage targets.

Facility/Rent Expense

The optimum level of rent expense is 4% to 7% of collections. Rent is a fixed cost, and if it is out of line, aside from renegotiating the lease, the dentist is probably not generating enough collections relative to the cost of the space the practice occupies. Again, this problem can be addressed in many ways. For example, if the office is only being used for a couple days of the week, the dentist may want to consider subletting the space to another dentist on days when the space is not otherwise in use.

Unfortunately, a common culprit where facilities expense is well over 7% of collections is the trappings trap. A long history of struggling dental practices bears testament to the fact that better space alone will not attract more patients. A fully developed plan for attracting and keeping new patients, as well as improved treatment acceptance among current patients, is the only way to increase the odds of practice growth. If such a plan is complemented by enhanced larger or updated space, then all the better.

Payroll

Payroll is the largest expense category in a dental practice and one that can very quickly balloon out of control or slowly eat up profits over a period of many years. Payroll should be between 20-22% of collections and payroll taxes should represent an additional 3-5%. Therefore, if a dentist's payroll costs are higher than 27% (note that total payroll costs for practices operating effectively with a ratio of two hygienists per dentist will exhibit an acceptable ratio of payroll to revenues, which ranges up to as high as 30%), the following may be at work in the practice:

• *There are too many employees.*
More staff does not guarantee an improvement in production, but does guarantee an increase in overhead.

• *Raises are based on longevity rather than productivity/ performance.*
Staff payroll expense in a dental office needs to be tied as closely as possible to the operating reality of the practice. Therefore, if production and collections are going down, payroll should not be increased. Dental practice owners should establish a compensation policy, which states that raises will be given based upon employee performance and the profitability of the practice.

• *The hygiene department's productivity is off.*
The ideal ratio of hygiene production relative to total practice production is between 25% and 30%. At this level of productivity,

the ratio of hygiene production to hygiene compensation is most likely to fall within the desired range of 2.5 and 3 to 1. When the ratio of hygiene production drops below 25% of total practice production, hygiene wages and, by extension, total staff wages will begin to inflate relative to total practice collections. Three reasons for low hygiene production are: 1) the hygienist has far more down time than should be the case, 2) patient retention is seriously lacking, and 3) periodontal treatment is minimal at best.

Hygienists
Obviously, the hygienist's salary can have a significant impact on the practice's bottom line. High hygiene compensation can tip the practice beyond the 22% staff wage benchmark (for practices operating with two hygienists per dentist, the staff wage benchmark can safely increase to 26%). If hygiene compensation is too low, the hygienist will likely be a "short-timer," leaving the dentist scrambling to fill the void. Some steps the dentist can take to ensure hygiene is a full contributor to total practice success are:

- Review hygiene production each month during the team's monthly meeting

- Customize the time per patient based on patient need, not on a rigid one-hour allocation for each patient

- Provide hygiene hours in the evening if patients are requesting late appointments

- Expect the hygienist to use the intra-oral camera, so patients can see the condition of their mouth every six months

- Expect the hygienist to review previously proposed treatments with the patients and encourage a continuance of the dentist's recommended treatment plan

- Expect the hygienist to speak positively about the dentist's professional abilities, recent continuing education accomplishments, or specific treatment cases (without referring to specific patients) that have been particularly impressive

- Expect the hygienist to educate the patient, not only on oral hygiene, but also on the array of practice services available

Laboratory

Depending on the thrust of the practice, laboratory expenses can represent anywhere from 8% to 14% of overhead; therefore, the size of laboratory expense can be very revealing as to the type of patient targeted and the focus of care delivery within a given practice. A dental practice with a large percentage of patients covered by managed care who require prosthetic dentistry will more than likely have a very high lab expense to collections percentage (i.e., 14% to 16%, or more) despite the fact that the dentist uses a laboratory that charges reasonable or low fees. Regarding so called "low cost labs," it is important to remember that the cost of lab work includes the cost associated with poor lab work, which requires frequent "remakes." Frequent remakes can also damage a patient's confidence and/or satisfaction with the dentist. An unhappy patient means the potential loss of future treatment revenues and referrals from that patient.

Dental Supplies

The optimal amount spent for dental supplies is 5% of collections. If total dental supply expense is higher than this, there may be problems in how these supplies are being purchased or handled, or items of expense such as continuing education and equipment repairs may have been reported in the wrong expense category. To keep the cost of supplies in check, many dentists have opted to deal directly with suppliers rather than ordering through catalogues. Local representatives for a supplier will often provide better service and keep the practice informed about sales. However, the supplier representative should never be allowed to sort through and fill a practice's store of supplies at random. All supplies should be kept in one place and accounted for with a sound inventory control system.

Several additional ways to keep a handle on supplies include comparative shopping and purchasing through a local co-op.

Other/Miscellaneous Expenses

Other expenses to consider include office supplies (which should not exceed 3% of total charges); telephone (no more than 1%); legal and accounting fees (no more than 2%); additional business expenses, such as dues, subscriptions and licenses (a total of 3%); payroll taxes (2%); and marketing/advertising (0.5% to 1%).

Practice Management Through Benchmarks and Statistics

There are five critical reports that each practice management system generates. These reports include Production by Provider and by Procedure Code Report, Collections Report, Accounts Receivable Report, Insurance Aging Report and Adjustment Report.

Comparative Analysis

While low on their list of favorite pastimes, all dentists know they should monitor the operational and financial health of their practice. Ignoring this management task will, at best, create problems that rob dentists of time and money and, at worst, result in the loss of their dental business. An effective management and business monitoring system will allow the owner/dentist to maintain the health of the practice, and have more time to treat patients. All numbers monitored should be:

1. Statistical interpretations of how well the dentist is achieving his or her vision and goals for the practice

2. Viewed in a daily, weekly, monthly and yearly context

3. Interpreted as a coherent story about the practice and its performance

The relationship of one number that counts to the other numbers is very important. Often dentists have certain comfort numbers that make them think they're successful. But, unless the dentist

---

sees the big picture comparing that one number with others, he may have a false sense of security. For example, a high collection percentage in one month may be the result of lower than usual collections in the prior month.

4. Shared with the Staff of the Practice
A dentist cannot function and performance goals cannot be met without the support of the staff of the practice. Therefore, the staff must also interpret the practice statistics. Sharing the practice statistics (not including individual salary figures) is a sign of trust and the only way to empower staff to be self-directed. Further, sharing the numbers will facilitate staff "buy-in" to corrective steps when and if required.

5. At the Base of Business Management Decisions
Management by supposition is like walking across the street blindfolded. Management by statistics removes the blindfold and allows the dentist to move confidently toward his or her goals.

6. Appreciated as Effective Practice Management Tools
A dentist should never think that emphasizing the profit of the practice is anathema to the practice of dentistry. When a dentist decides to purchase or start a dental practice, he or she has made a conscious decision to enter the business of dentistry. That decision comes with the responsibility for staying aware of the operational and financial health of the business by regularly monitoring statistical data generated by the business.

Practice Benchmarks
Financial and statistical benchmarks allow dentists to compare their individual practices to the norm. In other words, benchmarks are the equivalent of the image in a dental X-ray. Dentists should know what a normal image looks like so that they are prepared to diagnose any abnormalities and determine a course of corrective action. The following are financial benchmarks to consider. It is important to note that variations from these benchmarks may not be good or bad, but definitely are worth investigating.

Accounts Receivable

As noted previously, the overall rate of collections should be 98.5% or better. To achieve this, time is the key. The longer an account continues past due, the more likely it is that it will never be collected. A simple measure of the health of accounts receivable is shown in the example below. First, the daily collection rate is determined by dividing total collections by the number of days required to create the collections (365 for an annual report of collections, 180 days for a six-month statement of collections, etc.). The total of accounts receivable is then divided by the daily collections rate. The net result is the daily collections equivalent to total accounts receivable. The benchmark figure result desired should range between 30 and 45 days. The number of days for cosmetic and other elective treatment-focused practices should be 20 or less as the majority of compensation for services rendered should be collected at the time of treatment.

Accounts Receivable	
Total accounts receivable divided by total receipts divided by the number of days of the year elapsed through the date of the income statement. The target high for dental receipts is the equivalent of 30 to 45 days of receipts.	
Example:	
Accounts receivable as of December 31, 2006	$ 100,000
Total receipts as of December 31, 2006	$ 900,000
Days Receivable = $ 100,000/($ 900,000/365)	
Days Receivable = $ 100,000/$ 2,465.75	
Days Receivable = 40.56 days	

On a more detailed note, 95% of all patients should have paid all fees for services rendered to the practice within 60 days of treatment. After 90 days the likelihood that balances due will be paid drops to 20%. A target benchmark for receivables is for 70% of total patient accounts due to be paid in less than 30 days. Unfortunately, more than a few dental practices have a larger number of patient receivables that are more than 90 days overdue. These significantly past due accounts have a major impact on the ability of those practices to reach industry standard profitability. In terms of accounts due from insurance payors, there should be no balances past due 90 days or more.

Active Patients

A practice's potential can be roughly gauged by the number of active patients it has. The definition of an "active" patient ranges from one who has been in for treatment at least once in the last 18 months in an urban setting to one who has been seen within three years in a rural setting.

The typical solo practice has between 1,500 to 2,000 active patients (based on an active patient definition of 18 months). The benchmark for the average production per active patient per year in a general dentistry office is $300 to $500. Therefore, using a low-side figure of $350 in production per patient per year, a practice with 1,750 active patients should gross 1,750 x $350 = $612,500. Assume a practice is open four days for 48 weeks (or 192 days) per year. At eight hours per day, this represents 1,536 hours per year. The $612,500 divided by 1,536 hours equals about $400 per hour for the dentist and hygiene department to generate.

Dentist Service Mixture

Run the Production by Procedure Code report for a six-month period for each dentist in the practice. Total the production for procedures for each dentist that are equal to or higher than the fee for a crown. Divide the total of these procedures for each dentist into the total production per dentist. The desired result should be that 50% to 75% of dentist production is generated from these higher end procedures. Examples of these procedures are:

- Crown and Bridge Preparations
- Denture or Partial Impressions
- Cosmetic Bonding or Veneers
- Periodontal or Oral Surgery
- Root Canal

- Implant Procedures

- Orthodontic Banding

Recall Effectiveness

Recall effectiveness often is not calculated. Many practices pre-appoint their patients at their recall appointment for the next recall appointment and incorrectly assume that recall is doing fine because the hygiene schedule is full. Two methods by which recall effectiveness may be measured or assessed are:

1. Divide the number of active patients (those seen at least once during the last 18 months) by the average number of hygiene patients seen per month. An ideal result will be 9 to 1; if the result is higher than 9 to 1, the indication is that there is room for improvement in the recall program.

2. From the practice's Production by Procedure report, find the number of periodic exams (code 0120) completed in a six-month period. Then divide the periodic exam total by the number of the practice's active patients (those seen at least once during the last 18 months). The ideal result is 70% to 80%. A percentage of active patients to periodic exams above this amount indicates that there is room for improvement in the patient recall program.

Production Adjustment Report
- PPO Write-Offs

- Medicaid Write-Offs

- Courtesy Savings Write-Offs

- FOD — Friends of Dentist Write-Offs

- Professional Courtesy Write-Offs

- Staff Centered Care Write-Offs

- Charity Dental Care Write-Offs

Every practice should be able to generate a report that will show how much of the practice production is written off. However, the quality, thus functional value of this report is dependent upon the quality of the inputs. Most practice software allows for the categorization of write-offs so the dentist can better understand where the money is going. Some dentists reviewing this report for the first time are surprised to see that they are writing off roughly $15,000 in dentistry for friends and family per quarter, and others find the reports most useful in keeping up with the activities of their front desk by making sure that all write-offs are legitimate.

CHAPTER 10

Creating and Realizing Practice Value Through Practice Management

Relative to many forms of business operating in the U.S. today, the accounting and finances of a dental practice (i.e., the debits and credits of payables, receivables, inventory and cash deposits) are relatively simple. However, the business of managing staff, patient flow, scheduling, etc., of a dental business is among the most challenging of any business out there.

Dentists have it tough. They go to dental school to learn how to treat teeth and they get out and realize that they spend more time thinking about business matters such as managing staff, scheduling, marketing the practice and setting up systems than they do about caring for patients.

The human factor looms large in the business of dentistry. Dental practice owners are challenged daily with a complex mix of patient and staff personalities, aspirations, expectations, fears, concerns and general baggage. Yet, most navigate these waters and seem to enjoy their careers. This is because it's also one of the most satisfying and rewarding jobs if approached with the understanding and confidence that comes from a commitment to a solid plan and strategy.

This chapter is intended to shine some light on the natural emotions dentists and their staff experience when working together and those particularly unique personalities within a practice staff that can represent a danger to a practice family or be a blessing. In addition, it is the aim of this chapter to suggest some general direction as to how the often turbulent waters of a practice family can be negotiated, allowing new owners to realize value in the practice they recently started or purchased and existing owners to create value in their practices.

The New Owner

You've purchased or started your own practice and thus made a key investment in your future. This is what all those years in dental school were getting you ready for, and yet there are questions in the back of your mind. Are you nuts? How will you pull it off? Why do you feel so nervous? That's a lot of business debt to have borrowed! What if you fail? If you have asked yourself many of these same questions, relax, you're normal and that's a good start for running a successful practice.

Now that you know you're normal, here are some answers to these questions:

- *Are you nuts?*
Though some might think you are crazy for investing over $100,000 and four years to spend the rest of your working days with your hands in someone's mouth, you're definitely not nuts for wanting to own your own practice. It's the most satisfying way to practice, and it's evidence most dentists agree with, as the majority of dental professionals practice their trade as the sole licensed care provider in practices they wholly own.

- *How will you pull it off?*
Assuming you're not crazy and thoroughly researched the practice, looking to see what made it successful in the first place, and bought a healthy operation — keep an eye on what's already working well. Don't make big changes right away unless something or someone

is obviously not productive and healthy for the practice. Work with the existing staff and gain their confidence, and then they will help you gain the confidence of the patients. Put your stamp on the practice gradually, but keep some of what made it great intact. You don't have to wipe away all traces of the former owner to make it yours. Build on their legacy.

· *Why do you feel so nervous?*
A little tension keeps us on our toes, but you can't stand on your toes the whole day. Learn to relax into what you're doing at the moment. Keep your office manager in tune with what you're worrying about and what you're enjoying and let her help make it work for you. Don't spend every minute waiting for disaster or signs that you made a mistake. Build on everything that feels right and learn from everything that goes wrong. Enjoy these early days and develop a vision for where you want to go. Don't expect to step right into the shoes of the seasoned dentist whose practice you bought. Set yourself some attainable short-term goals. Achieving these near-term goals will build your confidence and give you focus. Don't wait for things to happen; plan for what you want and build it. Share your vision with your staff and give them the tools of confidence, respect and inclusion so that they'll see your dream and make it their mission.

· *What if you fail?*
Less than 0.5% of dentists flop in business, and if you do all the above you're not likely to fall into this very small group. Be a good person, do good dentistry, and treat people right, and your odds of experiencing success are better than 99 to 1.

Take the Helm

Your practice will either sink to the skill and comfort level of your staff, or rise to meet the standards you set. However, the practice can't rise to meet your standards without an increase in the skill and comfort level of the staff. It is up to you as the owner of the practice to make that happen.

For the dentist, leadership is a key linchpin in the ongoing success of the practice. When a dentist is an effective leader, there is positive staff attitude, low staff turnover and a more cohesive team with a greater job satisfaction ratio. Effective leadership is particularly important for new practice owners whose primary goal following the acquisition of the practice is winning over the staff and earning their trust and loyalty in a relatively short time frame.

Here are some guidelines that may prove helpful to the existing or new practice owner:

Assess Your Starting Position

Interview each staff person separately, learn their strengths, weaknesses and work style. Invite their insights about the former work environment. New owners should strive to not make changes in staff during their first six months in the practice to see how the team gels. However, if there is a problem person who is resistant from the very beginning, terminate them as soon as you are aware there is a problem because the reality is that a new person will hurt you less than an existing employee who is creating chaos. If there is an office manager, be sure to help her understand that she isn't the "shop steward," but rather the facilitator of the practice management vision. Dental office managers generally focus on the hands-on management process of the practice such as operating systems, organization, scheduling and sometimes task delegation. The implementation of these systems keeps the practice running. The leading dentist should be the one who manages the staff by knowing the strengths of those staff individuals.

Lead by Example

First and foremost, be honest. Instances of staff embezzlement frequently happen because the "leader" exhibits signs of dishonesty by pocketing cash or running some insurance scam. Set a good work ethic by being punctual when coming to the office and getting to your patient appointments. Treat people with respect. Live your mission and vision. Tackle difficult issues head-on; ignored problems only become larger. Act like a leader and make decisions. Even if it is difficult in the beginning, it will become easier with practice. Your staff will see you as a leader and respond accordingly.

Share Your Vision

Effective leaders help the staff see the big picture. They help staff interpret how the day-to-day activities create the practice vision by "living" the mission statement and "working" the practice program. Frequently, dentists are reluctant to share the numbers of the practice. As a general rule, if you are a good leader your team will want to share your vision and success. The more successful you are, the more successful the practice. By sharing the numbers of the practice with the staff, they can see clearly the favorable impact of their contribution to that success story. Everyone wants to be a winner! Help your staff to increase their skill levels. Strong leaders both encourage and challenge their staff to advance their skill levels, support that commitment and provide an environment that makes success a reality.

Communication Skills

"Listen more and talk less" are great words of advice to us all and to staff leaders in particular. When the leader listens to the staff, the result is a growth in their sense of trust in leadership, safety in their staff positions, and ownership of their individual job responsibilities and the day-to-day issues of the practice. Staff members who feel free to communicate with you directly will take ownership for the pursuit of solutions to problems within the practice. When you are communicating with the staff, speak clearly and directly with a sense of assuredness when making your points, and make use of open-ended questions. Where appropriate, it is always good to wrap up discussions by summarizing and setting an action plan to achieve goals.

Motivate with the Positive

Catch your staff doing something right, then use positive language to praise them. Speak positively as a matter of habit. Create a culture for positive emotions and expectations in your office. There truly is such a thing as a self-fulfilling prophecy, and most people by nature want to live up to your expectations. People are motivated by different things and it is not always necessarily money, but more frequently, praise.

Be Results Oriented

The effectiveness with which you lead will determine the type of staff team you have working for you. Excellent leaders attract, expect, nurture and keep excellent staff. Learn to spot the differences between being busy and being productive. Being productive is not only more effective, but much more rewarding. If your staff has the right aptitude and attitude for success, provide them with the training necessary to achieve your vision. If not, hire staff that does.

Learning effective leadership skills will result in a positive employee culture, which in turn will result in a well-run practice, improved profitability and increased practice value. For new practice owners, effective leadership represents the foundation on which a smooth transition and future growth will be realized.

Barriers to Effective Staff Management

Fear

When confronting a problem employee, their reaction may very well mirror the problem you have been having with them, but you can't afford to let fear of their reaction freeze you into inactivity. If they leave the practice, there may be some dramatics, but it will only last a short while and the benefits of their absence will be long lasting. If they bad mouth you in the community, stay calm and true to who you are. People are smart and will come to see through their act. In regard to patient gossip, remember those that gossip make a practice of gossiping about something all the time; you're just the flavor of the day.

If someone on your staff is causing the irritation and disintegration of your stomach lining, hold them accountable. Let them know that they must start doing as you ask or they will be asked to leave. That's fair. And there's nothing to be afraid of.

Victim Mentality

You may feel that everyone wants something from you and nobody cares about how you feel. What can you do to end this misery? This victim mentality is the result of isolated thinking. Teams rarely think this way because they look at the big picture. A victim looks inward and only sees their side of the story. A team member looks inward on a regular basis to make sure they are doing everything they can to make things work. Then they look around to see who needs something they can help with and who is doing something great that they can compliment. Team members notice how fantastic their team is and consider how grateful, proud and lucky they feel to be a part of it. A victim mentality is incompatible with a teamwork atmosphere.

A Key Source of Practice Management Support

An office manager can be a key source of support to the new owner in a practice transition. All too often, the absence of support from the office manager results in the loss of support from the staff in general. However, exactly how the manager fits into the picture will depend on the role she has played in the practice and the role she wants to play in welcoming a new dentist.

If the office manager is one who really handles most administrative duties in the practice, she can be invaluable in helping everything progress smoothly for all parties. After all, she has her heart in two countries, so to speak. She still feels loyalty and friendship for the dentist she's been working with (the seller), and whether he's staying on or retiring, she wants the best for him. Now there's another person (the buyer) who will play a part in her future, and she wants to help, and make the new dentist feel welcome.

One of the most effective ways that an office manager can help a new owner/dentist through the transition process is to talk him or her up with enthusiasm and confidence to the staff of the practice, noting that there is nothing threatening for them in this new change and that the new dentist doesn't want to come in and fire the staff or make their lives miserable. He or she just wants to be accepted, made to feel a part of the team and supported.

How to Build a Great Team

Think back to when you set up your dental practice. You didn't take anything for granted, you researched the equipment you needed to buy and bought the best you could afford. You knew that these would be the tools you would use every day to make your practice successful, so you wanted to be sure they suited you. The same focus and effort is required to build a great staff. These are the people you will work with every day, therefore they must be well-suited to you.

When hiring staff, define the person who will suit you in each position to be filled, and then look for that person in the people you interview. When hiring an office manager, you need to think about what an office manager is supposed to do and what you expect from the position. When hiring a dental hygienist, you need to determine whether your hygienist is to function as a part of the team, or does she come in, clean teeth and go home.

It is also important to identify desired traits for each position and then start out with someone that shows promise in terms of having and further developing those. Take a carefully considered and purposeful approach to hiring staff because hiring the wrong people will hurt you, the other employees and your patients. The stress from a really bad hire can even ripple out to your family, and your staff's families.

Prepare to be patient and wait for the right person. Don't hire a project; you have enough to do already. Be very clear about your expectations and the responsibilities of the position. Ask open-ended questions and listen to the candidate's answers and to your instincts. Observe their response and their ability to articulate their thoughts, their grammar, and look for insights into their character.

If a candidate has poor grammar, you may think it won't bother you, but remember the way they talk to you in the interview is the way they will talk to your patients. If they do not connect well or don't sound intelligent, that's what your patients and staff will experience. Hiring a staff member who is a poor fit with the rest of the staff can cost you a good staff member in a few months.

Once the right person for the job is hired, they should start work with a basic job description that can grow as they grow in their position. You should clearly state your expectations for them and provide them with goals. From that point forward it is important that corrective guidance be provided in a timely manner and those achievements be recognized and celebrated, as the success of team members is your success as well. Salaries should be a product of local industry standards tempered by individual abilities.

The Ideal Front Desk Team Member

The front desk person is there, first and foremost, to make a great first and last impression on every patient who visits the practice. She exhibits a warm and sincere manner on the phone as the first patient contact is usually made by phone. She makes decisions based on what the patient communicates, and asks questions to clarify the patient's needs. She keeps her cool as she juggles calls with patient arrivals. She exhibits patience and tenacity in dealing with insurance claims and the inevitable delays in reimbursement that occur. She shows nerve and conviction, tempered by graciousness, in asking patients to pay their fee.

The Ideal Dental Assistant Team Member

The dental assistant is there to serve your patients and make your day go smoothly. She is organized and gets her "behind the scenes" work done and really listens to her patients. She sees other assistants as team members, and wants to share what she knows with them in order to make the team stronger. She cares about the practice, she doesn't gossip, and works steadily, not worrying about whose responsibility it is. She's thorough, as she checks charts, makes sure the right anesthetic is being used, and ensures the care being delivered matches with that which was scheduled.

The Ideal Hygienist Team Member

The development and maintenance of a strong recall program is fundamental to a successful hygiene program, and a strong recall program requires a group effort from every member of the staff. Therefore, the ideal hygienist is team focused and thus hard to pick out from the rest of the staff. She can be seen cleaning up the lab, washing dishes in the break room, helping the assistants finish cleaning rooms, and generally participating as a member of the team whose support she needs so dearly.

Guiding a Great Team

Every team will eventually get off track and the leader will have to pull them back in line. When this happens to you, the best thing to do is determine what is wrong and what needs to happen to make things right again. Speak clearly and directly in explaining just how the team has gotten off course, and how they will be able to pull back together again. Letting them keep their dignity in the face of your disapproval will benefit everyone and get you the results you desire faster. It's worth it to take the time you need to cool down and consider the best way to proceed to get the outcome you want.

Respect and trust are the foundation and glue that hold any great team together. Where there is an erosion of either of these critical factors, swift action needs to be taken.

Respect

Respect needs to be the foundation of every relationship. Therefore, because it's hard to respect someone who doesn't respect you, it's not advisable to hold on to a staff member who doesn't respect the boss.

A respected employee doesn't dwell as much on whether their salary is fair. An employee who doesn't feel respected has no other gauge than money. Your employees really want to feel cared about, considered and respected. You may be able to hang on to an employee for a while by offering raises in place of respect, but that approach will only last until you are unable to justify further raises or the employee decides it's not about the money, and moves on. Solid professional relationships grounded in genuine respect, consideration and mutual admiration build the ties that bind a dental team together.

Trust

Your patients like entering a healthy office environment in which the staff gets along well, is happy, and genuinely likes what they're doing. Trust is the foundation of a healthy office environment. An environment of trust virtually eliminates gossip, and fosters effective teamwork and coopcration.

The most effective dental teams exhibit a great deal of trust among team members. This includes the staff's trust in your commitment to do the right thing as a licensed professional dentist and as the owner of the business. Your staff needs to have confidence in your commitment to be fair and to respect them.

Clearly, when it comes to trust, what's good for the staff goes double for the dentist. You have to be able to trust your people. However, there will be times when you feel your trust has been violated. The good news is that, if dealt with swiftly, this type of situation can represent an excellent opportunity to reinforce in the minds of your staff, the importance you place upon trust within the office.

If you have a team member that you just don't trust, you probably need to let him or her go. To do otherwise is to run the risk of undermining trust throughout your practice as your message regarding the importance of trust gets lost in a blur of conflicting signals impacting your staff.

Identifying and Dealing with Problem Staff Member Profiles

· *Niceness As a Cover*

There are people who use "niceness" to cover something up. It may be inadequate skills, laziness, a passive/aggressive personality, etc. Odd as it may seem to some, dealing with the "big teddy bear" in the practice can represent quite a challenge. One common characteristic of "sweet" employees is they feel very threatened when faced with constructive criticism. It seems they count so strongly on getting by on sweetness, that, when it fails, they don't have anything to fall back on. Asking them to look inside themselves for the will to change or improve seems so difficult because they are worried they don't really have what it takes to succeed in this job. When confronted many will quit rather than persevere, and thus end up doing you a favor by opening up the opportunity to find someone who will do the job well.

· *The Invisible Bully*
Bullies are sneaky. They usually don't show their true colors in front of the boss. To the boss they can often come across as very knowledgeable (and sometimes they are), hard-working, and put upon. However, nothing can disturb the peace of a practice more than a bully.

If and when a bully is identified, you will find that some can be tamed. In fact, they may not even realize they are taking over and shutting everyone else down. If so, giving them some ideas on how to respect and draw out the views of others may solve the problem. On the other hand, if they become aggressive or abusive when presented with the need to change for the sake of the team, it may be impossible to get them with the program. Don't try to change a bully who intimidates and is aggressive, as you'll just be wasting your time and wear the rest of the team down.

If you made a mistake and hired a bully, let them go. Keeping a bully on board is asking too much of everyone who has to try to function around them. Don't worry about unemployment; pay it. Your staff is watching and hoping you'll do the right thing.

· *The Pile Driver*
Though you may see signs of the pile driver personality in one of your chair side assistants or front desk administrators, this personality most often crops up in the office manager position.

The office manager in a practice accepts a huge amount of responsibility. Sometimes office managers may feel like responsibility is always building and they are always under pressure to perform. Many are guilty of seeing everyone else's failure as their own — in other words, they are too heavily invested. Though seemingly noble, the downside to this extreme level of emotional, mental and physical commitment can be the creation of a controlling and insensitive office manager. She may start to look at the staff as a bunch of slackers who would stand in the kitchen eating all day if it weren't for her. She may look at patients as ungrateful losers who don't care about what their broken appointment does to "her" schedule. She can become demanding, demeaning and controlling.

The owner can help an office manager who has gotten off track by sitting down and talking about it. State the problem and ask her how she intends to fix it. Rather than feeling that you have to come up with a solution, this approach forces her to take responsibility and gives her the opportunity to show you she understands and cares about your concern.

Effective Time Management

People tend to equate busy with productive, but we have all observed that a busy schedule does not always equate to a productive day's work. In fact, most of us have all the time we need, but make poor use of the time we have.

That's why it's so important for your scheduler to understand the daily, weekly, monthly and yearly goals for the practice. It is possible and desirable to work at a relaxed, enjoyable pace and still meet your production goals. That's the most satisfying way to work, and with the dedication and determination of the scheduler, it is achievable. Take a look at the way you work in your office, individually and as a team. Take a look at your personal life as well. Where are you spending it? Life goes by quickly and we only get one shot at it. Make the most of it by making yourself aware of what you are doing.

CHAPTER 11

Retirement Planning

Retirement may be the furthest thing from the mind of a young dentist just starting out or a mid-career dentist enjoying the rewards of building a successful practice. Yet, it is a given in the industry that less than 10% of dentists will be able to retire at age 65 and maintain the lifestyle to which they are accustomed. The other 90% may have to push back their retirement date, work part time during their "golden years," or reduce their standard of living during a retirement phase that could last 30 years or more.

Why do so many dentists lack the wherewithal to retire when they wish? After all, dentists make a relatively great living. Part of the answer is their high levels of annual income are matched by high levels of outgo. Another part is that many dentists do not take a purposeful approach to business and the accumulation of wealth.

Retirement Planning

The cost of starting to save just twelve years later is losing two doublings of your money before you retire! That can be the difference between having $500,000 or $2 million!

The purpose of this book is to help YOU and other dentists focus on building wealth in your practice, so you can live the good life both during and after your professional career.

For those dentists who can and choose to, retirement means change, and this results in some experience of loss, which can bring on anxiety. Therefore, typical initial reaction to the prospect of retirement is a feeling of anxiety. To retire successfully, dentists must put any feelings of loss in perspective. This is best done through the clarification of their identity as being who they are rather than what they do. There is a trick to the graceful exit. It begins with recognizing when a job, a life stage, or a relationship is over, and then letting it go. It means leaving what is over without denying its validity or its past importance to our lives. It involves a sense of future, a belief that every exit brings us to a new point of entry and that we are moving on, rather than out.

A recently retired dentist was overheard grumbling, "In retirement you need a monthly income of 110% of your former monthly salary." Apparently, he had found out that retirement means having a lot more time on his hands to spend money. It costs something to travel, eat at fine restaurants and see movies. It even costs something to sit around and do nothing.

Concern about adequate income during retirement begins with the supposition that individuals will live for several years past their retirement age, that is, past the point of leaving the labor force. With the number of dentists approaching the age of retirement at historic highs, the question of how they will meet their retirement income needs looms large.

Can You Afford to Retire?

If retirement is not mandatory, the first question to answer before the practice is sold is, "How do I know if I have enough money to retire?" Presently, to retire in reasonable comfort, a dentist needs roughly $2 million in a qualified plan. Is this the absolute minimum? No, of course not! It depends on one's personal circumstances, objectives and temperament. But, for a reasonably comfortable retirement, it's a realistic number, at least for now.

To determine your unique retirement income needs, and thus the size of the retirement fund required, you need to do some analysis. A protocol for planning retirement should include the following:

Determine the Total of Your Personal Expense Needs in Retirement for One Year

- Calculate on a monthly basis what is spent on food, housing, gas, utilities, medical expenses, medical insurance, car insurance, entertainment, clothing, gifts, golf, travel, etc. (use last year's checkbook and credit card bills as aids).

- Include income tax payments and replacement of major items, such as an auto or a new roof (for example, if you spend $35,000 on a car and keep it for seven years, add $5,000 per year for auto; if a roof costs $6,000 and is replaced every 15 years, add $400 a year for a roof).

- Be realistic about how money is spent. Most people travel more in retirement.

- Total all of the above expenses and multiply by 12 to determine your yearly retirement income needs.

Determine Retirement Income for One Year

Choose your option: After retirement, a) "Do I plan to live strictly off of the income from investments, leaving the principal for emergencies or estate beneficiaries?" or b) "Do I plan to live on a combination of the income and principal of investments?"

If the answer is a) "Live on the income and leave the principal," add up the following:

- Yearly income from present taxable investments

- Income from IRAs and Social Security

- Income from money invested from the practice sale (for example, the practice is sold for $300,000; after payment of the

15% capital gains tax, $255,000 is invested in an instrument paying 5%, which yields $12,750 in interest per annum)

• The total of those three streams of income equals yearly income

If the answer is b) "Live on income and principal:"

• Calculate future income from Social Security, current taxable investments, IRAs, and principal and interest earned on the investment of the proceeds from the practice sale over one's life expectancy (this is a relatively complex process which is most likely best entrusted to a certified public accountant or certified financial planner).

Secret to Successful Retirement Planning Is Simple

• Don't wait until you can afford to put money away to start saving
• Saving becomes more expensive and more difficult the longer you wait

• Subtract total annual retirement living expense needs from total annual retirement income to determine retirement options.

• If the yearly income is larger than planned annual retirement expenditures, then congratulations! If expenditures are larger than annual retirement income, keep on working and save at a pace that will allow for retirement at a targeted point in the future. Another viable option is to sell the dental practice now and work at a reduced pace for the buyer as an associate so long as the practice will support two dentists.

When you know how much will be needed to meet your financial needs in retirement, a practice transition professional can structure and time the transition to best suit those needs. As is the case in many things, nothing good will come from delaying to make a plan. A common response from the average mature dentist when asked about transition or retirement plans is, unfortunately, "I'm going to do something in five years." In other words, most mature dentists plan to put their mind to their retirement and the ultimate transition of their practice only a few months before they want out.

So You Don't Have a Qualified Retirement Plan Yet?

Let's consider a common problem among dentists: You are earning a reasonable amount of money in your dental practice. You know that a retirement plan is needed, and you have identified an IRS-qualified retirement plan as a seemingly excellent tool for accumulating retirement savings with pre-tax dollars. Then you meet with a consultant in this area who tells you that an IRS-qualified retirement plan dictates that the employer cannot discriminate against the employees. In other words, the employees must have the same coverage as the dentist. After carefully reviewing the studies prepared by the consultant, and realizing that a large share of the total annual deductible contribution will need to be allocated to your employees, you decide that the practice can't afford a retirement plan at this time.

Stop! Don't write off a plan yet. Instead, use eligibility requirements available in the structuring of IRS qualified retirement plans (such as date of birth, years of service, job classification, and other areas of testing) to determine who does not have to be included in the plan. Rather than starting with the theory of "who must be included" in the plan, develop a plan that meets all discrimination tests, but works with the reverse concept of "who does not have to be included."

IRS-qualified retirement plans are not rigid products designed for the ease of IRS review. Rather, they are available to be customized, within limits, to give business owners the ability and incentive to save for retirement. Further, these plans allow business owners to build up savings which are immune from creditors, accumulate interest and dividend income and growth on a tax-deferred basis, and act as their own trustee in making all the investment decisions of the retirement plan. It is important to talk to an advisor who knows how to design a qualified retirement plan in such a manner that the annual contributions are maximized.

The Changing Retirement Model

Using the previously noted recently retired dentist (we will assume he retired in 2002) who was overheard grumbling, "In retirement you need a monthly income of 110% of your former monthly salary," and the American Dental Association's finding of $174,350 as the average net income for an independent private practitioner who owned all or part of his or her practice in 2002, retirement savings sufficient to support an annual gross retirement income need of over $190,000 would have been required. Assuming an investment return of 8% on retirement savings, a dentist needing $190,000 per annum and not wishing to deplete the corpus of his savings would need to have accumulated an income-producing nest egg totaling $2,375,000.

The findings in a 1995 American Dental Association survey, in which dentists were asked questions about their plans to finance their retirement, tended to support the previously noted claim that only four out of 100 dentists are financially able to retire at 65. The survey revealed that the majority of dentists whose primary occupation was private practice reported saving an average of only 10.5% of their income specifically for retirement. Using the previously mentioned $174,350 average net income per private practitioner, the annual savings would presently total $17,435. At this rate of savings, it would a take a dentist roughly 38 years to accumulate the equivalent of $2,375,000 in future inflation-adjusted dollars. Given the critical factor of compounding interest in achieving growth in savings, the assumption of 38 years is largely dependent upon a dentist reaching the median income for dentists shortly after graduating from dental school and then immediately initiating a retirement savings plan. This does not typically happen. It takes time for a dentist to position himself or herself to generate this type of income, and the early years of their career are dominated by debt repayment and accumulation of furniture, autos, housing, etc. Unfortunately, the average dentist does not begin to save in earnest until many years after graduating from dental school. This explains why so few dentists can truly afford to pursue an "idle retirement" when they reach 65.

Analytical data such as this is commonly referred to by retirement fund managers looking to motivate dentists to increase their annual retirement savings through "fear," and why not, their business is managing money. What is the best way to take the wind out of the sails of someone selling "fear?" Concede the point and then ask the question, "So what?"

As noted, during the prime working years of life, dentists have realized an average annual income far greater than the median income of working Americans. In retirement, despite all the previously noted doom and gloom facts and figures, dentists will realize a far greater retirement income than the average retired American. Dentists will do this by way of the extremely portable and flexible nature of their trade skill.

Idle Retirement

In 1881, when 19th Century German Chancellor Otto von Bismarck was inventing his pension system, he set the age for retirement at 65. At the time, very few people lived that long. Today, age 65 still dictates our views about work and retirement, even though life expectancies have almost doubled. Case in point, Robert J. Myers, one of the architects of the U.S. Social Security system, began his career in government service in 1934 as a member of the actuarial team for Social Security, and was the system's chief actuary from 1947 to 1970. He "did the math" that led to fixing Social Security's age of eligibility to receive full benefits at 65. This number, which has come to define "old age" for everyone now living in this country, had no previous biological, social or legal significance to Americans. Sixty-five was selected because, as Myers explained, "Sixty was too young and 70 was too old. So, we split the difference." What all this means is that longevity and retirement age have no correlation.

Irrespective of any debate over what the appropriate retirement age is, there is no doubt that the concept of an "idle retirement" is relatively new in the history of civilized man. As recently as the middle of the 19th century, the United States was largely an agrarian society, and individuals worked on the family farm for as long as they were able, while those who were not able to work stayed at home and were supported by their families. Life expectancy in 1850 was about 38 years at birth and about 28 years for 40-year-olds. The concept of retirement — at least as we know it today — barely existed.

Toward the end of the 19th century, the center of work life began to move away from farms and into the major industrial centers of the Northeast and Midwest. As was true on the farm, the need for retirement plans among these early factory pioneers was limited. Life expectancy at the turn of the 20th century was approximately 49 years at birth and about 12 years for those age 60. Workers continued to work for as long as they were able. Few employers provided retirement benefits — in fact, employer benefits of any type were uncommon. Benefits that did exist took the form of benevolent associations of workers, providing a common pool of funds to assist those in need due to death or disability. Often workers in a given location or industry were immigrants from the same country; the benevolent associations were their means of sticking together and helping their fellow immigrants. Those who did leave the workforce, typically because they were no longer able to work, survived on the generosity of their friends, family and neighbors, and their church or similar charitable assistance.

In the mid-1930s, when the Social Security system was established, life expectancy was about 60 years at birth and about 12 years for those age 60. With the Social Security retirement age set at 65, the system would typically pay benefits for only a few years. Similarly, when many employers and unions began introducing pension plans in the 1950s and 1960s, the retirement age generally was 65, while life expectancy was less than 70 years at birth and those age 65 could expect to live another 14 years.

Life expectancy in the United States today at birth is 76 years, while those currently age 65 can expect to live an additional 18 years. As a result, retirement benefits — both Social Security and employer-provided plans — that in the past were expected to provide benefits for a few years must now provide benefits for many years.

In the years to come, the percentage of the population aged 65 years and older will continue to grow. In fact, the fastest growing proportion of the population is those aged 85 years and older. This trend, like many trends in the latter half of the 20th century, is fueled by the baby boomer generation (those born between 1945 and 1964). Baby boomers are getting older and many are beginning to reach retirement age. To continue their preferred lifestyle and current standard of living, baby boomers will need substantial amounts of income throughout their retirement years. For many, this seems a near unachievable challenge given the current model for retirement.

The Three-Legged Stool

The current model retirement income is essentially a "three-legged stool" with the legs being Social Security, employer retirement benefits and personal savings income. Absent any other form of support, the stool is not likely to stand on just two legs, given the income demands of an idle retiree and longevity. In other words, absent income from retirement benefits or personal retirement savings, pursuit of idle retirement for most is virtually impossible. This means that an increasing number of older Americans are faced with the need to continue to work at some level, or run the risk of running out of retirement income before their death. A major change in the three-legged stool retirement model is required.

More and more, healthy older go-getters are opting for work over scrimping and saving in an idle retirement. By 2015, estimates the

National Council on the Aging, 20% of the U.S. work force will be over the age of 55, up from 13% in 2000. A fourth leg has been added to the stool.

The 2003 U.S. National Brain Drain Survey research by the SDG indicates that the values of younger people, especially those 25 years and younger, contribute to a natural tendency to want to leave the nest and experience new places and new people. However, maintaining close ties with family and friends, as well as having an affinity for familiar places, are also valuable and seem to remain important as people get older. Survey results indicated a sincere appreciation for hometown and small town values. In a society where many people tend to migrate to the coast, the mountains or to warmer southern states, 58% of the respondents liked the geographic location, climate and physical features of their hometowns, and nearly 50% agreed that adequate recreational and social opportunities exist in their hometowns.

Data for the Del Webb Baby Boomer survey of anticipated post retirement activity revealed that the majority (59%) of younger boomers (age 41-49) intend to buy a new home for their retirement and remain within driving distance of family members. Respondents over 45 years old with college educations are looking favorably at their hometowns as relocation options. As noted, the data shows numerous qualities of America's hometowns that make them a viable relocation option for baby boomers. It also shows that as many as 35% of individuals in this age group would like to start a business in their hometowns.

Returning baby boomers represent a significant cultural and economic resource for small hometowns. Technology-savvy respondents to the Del Webb Baby Boomer survey see opportunities for continued education, staying close to family and friends and holding leadership positions among the benefits their hometowns can provide. Some even see opportunities to grow and advance their careers.

It seems that in semi-retirement, baby boomers will shape the American workplace and compensate for a severe talent gap in rural/small town America due to a shrinking supply of new workforce entrants. In short, the addition of wages in semi-retirement as a fourth leg to the stool will allow baby boomers to fill their retirement income gap by engaging in work they enjoy where they want to enjoy it.

The Implications for Retiring Dentists

Dentists are not immune to these retirement trends, but their career choice does provide them with two significant advantages when it comes to meeting their retirement income needs. First, dentists are trained in a skill that is both in high demand and extremely portable. Second, they have a great deal of flexibility in their work hours. Therefore, with the re-emergence of the trend toward some level of work after 65, these two advantages afford dentists the opportunity to meet their retirement income needs with comparative grace and style.

In the 1960s and 1970s, when a greatly increased number of dentists were educated and unleashed on the market, a number of those newly minted professionals returned to the rural markets of their birth and upbringing where their parents and their spouses' parents still lived. Since beginning their careers, this group of dentists has in general accumulated retirement funds and personal wealth well in excess of their peers with practices in major metropolitan areas due to lower overhead, less competition, etc. However, as they reach retirement, their rural market location makes it difficult to sell their practices due to the limited number of young dentists (the traditional pool from which buyers emerge) interested in working in a rural market. Interestingly, many rural market practice owners find this phenomenon of no consequence since they have accumulated retirement savings sufficient to meet their retirement income needs, thus, simply walking away from the practice is an economically feasible, if not emotionally pleasing, option. Still others have little concern about the ability to sell their practices, since they intend to continue working as long as they are physically able.

In general, those dentists who settled in major metropolitan markets have found it more difficult to accumulate wealth outside of their practice during the course of their careers because of the increased cost of living, higher practice overhead, etc. However, they are blessed with the ability to attract the interest of numerous buyers once they put their practices on the market. In fact, in most instances, dentists in major metropolitan markets are able to sell their dental practices for the maximum the practices' historical cash flow will support (75% of annual collections on average). The problem is, a larger number of dentists in major metropolitan markets find that, although they may be able to sell their dental businesses for top dollar, the total of their retirement savings is still insufficient to meet their retirement income needs.

The "Green Acres" Retirement Solution

As noted, rural market and suburban/metropolitan market dental practice owners have diametrically opposed blessings and curses when it comes to retirement and the sale of their practices. However, by taking advantage of the portable and flexible nature of their chosen careers, rural and major metropolitan market dentists can work together to meet their retirement needs and ideals.

Like the findings of the Del Webb Baby Boomer Survey, many major metropolitan market dentists and their spouses may be very interested in retiring to an environment offering a slower pace of life, reduced cost of living, greater buying power in terms of land and housing, greater access to outdoor sports and entertainment such as fishing, boating, hunting and ranching, and being closer to family and old friends. Therefore, purchasing the dental practice of a dentist in a small town/rural market at a significant discount relative to the price received for their suburban/metropolitan practice could easily make up any deficiency in retirement income through a combination of reduced cost of living and part-time earned income.

From the perspective of the rural market dentist, this strategy affords a buyer where few if any would have otherwise existed. With the buyer in place, the rural market dentist may either retire from dentistry entirely or negotiate to continue working in the practice as an associate on days the new owner is not in the office.

From the perspective of the consumer of dental care in rural markets, it's all good. They continue to have access to dental care provided by professionals possessing a huge degree of clinical experience and expertise.

So there it is, the "Green Acres" retirement strategy. Problem: "Insufficient retirement income." Solution: "Implementation of a strategy to leverage the portable/flexible nature of a career in dentistry to fill the income gap." Collateral benefits include, but are not necessarily limited to, increased demand for rural market practices and improved prospects for those in need of dental care in rural markets.

Death, Disability and Crisis Planning

No one likes to think about an untimely death or disabling accident, but the stark reality is that failing to plan for such an occurrence can leave loved ones in dire straits. Your family should not have to worry about making mortgage payments and paying other bills in their time of grief. Having a solid plan in place will bring peace of mind not only to you but to those at home and in your office.

What Happens When the Dentist Dies or Is Disabled?

When a practicing dentist dies or is seriously disabled, there usually is a brief grace period during which the family, staff and patients are grieving. Then the staff reports back to work and the phones resume ringing. The surviving spouse usually is so caught up in sorrow and handling the funeral or disability care arrangements that it is extremely difficult for him or her to focus on dealing with the many details of operating and selling the practice.

There are usually two choices of where to turn for assistance:

- A family attorney, accountant, relative or key staff member who offers to assist the spouse in trying to sell the practice
- A dental practice broker who was identified by the dentist prior to his death or disability

---

Managing the Risk of Death or Disability

Without a plan, a surviving spouse's only option is to sell the practice by herself or himself:

Advantages	Disadvantages
• Save on brokerage fee	• No skill in selling or evaluating a business
	• Often lacks knowledge about operation of practice
	• Normally has little or no access to qualified buyers
	• Unskilled in negotiations
	• Decline in value

Four key questions to be answered at this time are:

- What should we do about the patients who are scheduled for treatment?
- What should we do about patients who are receiving treatment and whose procedures are not completed?
- What should we do about disposing of the practice?
- To whom can we talk about the situation and what should we tell them?

Managing the Risk of Death or Disability

With a plan, the surviving spouse's options include the use
of a practice broker:

- Experienced in practice sales
- Knowledgeable in the current market environment for dental
  practices
- Has qualified buyers
- Has financing resources
- Draft copies of necessary documents
- Immediate reaction without delay (peace of mind)

In some instances, the spouse and/or staff have been contacted by
parties interested in purchasing the practice, so two more questions
go on the list: "How should we respond to such queries?" and "What
is the practice worth?"

As word spreads of the dentist's death or disability, usually there are
several calls to the office or to the surviving spouse from dentists
interested in buying the practice. Most of these initial calls are from
dentists who believe they may be able to purchase the practice for a
significantly reduced price — and for good reason. The clock is the
enemy in these situations, and the value of the practice decreases
as time ticks away.

Death and Disability Planning

Smart investors protect themselves and their families from the
volatility of the stock market by planning their investments through
diversification. It is equally important for dentists to plan for their
families' protection if the unexpected happens. Dentists who die or
become disabled without a plan for such events put their patients,
staff and families in a difficult spot.

It is typical during the first month for the spouse of a deceased or
disabled dentist to do little or nothing regarding the practice due to

grief. Others, including the family attorney, may become involved, but normally they are not well-versed in dental practice sales and approach the matter with an inadequate sense of urgency. The critical period for the sale of a practice, in the case of the owner's death or permanent disability, is the first 30 to 45 days after the event. The practice should ideally be sold within this time frame, because after then it can rapidly begin to lose value.

With a death and disability planning program in place, immediate efforts will be set in motion to initiate the sales process. This can be done because most of the necessary documentation will already be in the possession of the practice-transition broker who was identified by the dentist prior to death or disability and who was provided with prearranged authority from the dentist to sell the practice. (See Chapter 4 for more detailed information about a practice broker's actions in such circumstances.)

Preparations for the possible death and/or disability of a dental practice owner include:

- Membership in a mutual assistance group (discussed in greater detail in the next section of this chapter)
- A well-thought-out emergency plan for the practice
- A current will that addresses the management and ultimate sale of the practice
- A durable power of attorney
- The addition of the practice owner's spouse as an authorized signer on the practice deposit account(s)
- A letter of instruction to the spouse and staff
- Pre-selection of a transition specialist/broker

Mutual Assistance Groups

A mutual assistance group is normally composed of six to 12 individual dentists who agree to work a member's practice in the case of death or disability. Although these groups are extremely useful and provide a critical function in keeping a practice active and productive, it is usually not in their area of expertise to market and sell a dental practice. Consequently, they provide an immediate function to fill in for the deceased or disabled member, but marketing and selling the practice are still major issues that should be handled by a good dental practice broker.

Steps that a mutual assistance group can take to increase its effectiveness include:

- *Prepare as a Group*
Each practitioner should advise the group concerning his or her choice of practice-transition agents. In addition, an experienced, local and active practice broker should occasionally be invited to visit with the group. Some groups invite spouses and/or estate advisers to organizational meetings. The best brokers for crisis incidents are those who maintain a database of purchasers who have previously signed confidentiality forms and are eager to purchase if the right opportunity presents itself. The best brokers will also be capable of advising the group about the transition process and provide some idea about practice values and timing expectations in the case of emergency.

- *Select a Group Leader*
Choose one group leader for each practice that will be supported. The contact person can be a source of comfort and communication for the practice staff, the family and the practice agents (attorneys, accountants and, of course, the broker). Some mutual assistance groups designate one dentist who will be the director in the event of any crisis. Other groups choose a different dentist for each practice, because he or she is a personal friend or confidant of that particular family.

- *Set Realistic Group Expectations*
Most assistance groups agree to work gratuitously in the practice for two or three months. The group should not be expected to manage the practice for an unrealistic length of time. The practice

schedule is usually reduced so that each group member can satisfy his or her obligation by visiting the practice a minimum of one time per week. The practitioner's estate or spouse should be advised before the commencement of professional effort that reasonable compensation will be a requirement after that amount of time.

• *Write Down Directions*

Each member should leave directions so that their respective practices will be priced competitively and attractively. When a professional career-ending crisis occurs, the practice needs to be sold or discontinued in a timely manner. Some purchasers expect or are advised by inexperienced agents that the goodwill of the practice is always greatly diminished immediately after the owner leaves. However, if a competent and stable staff is present, the operating systems are up to date, the location is attractive, and the leasehold improvements are modern, the practice value may continue for an extended period of time. Unfortunately, it is probably wise to be somewhat compromising about the value of the practice in a crisis-motivated sale. The mutual assistance group intermediary can assist the estate or spouse in making realistic decisions about his or her practice-sale expectations.

• *Establish Performance Expectations*

Discuss the group's professional performance expectations. Some group members may prefer not to perform particular operative disciplines. The group leader should define the responsibilities of the group's members, both collectively and individually. Additionally, in order to preserve practice's goodwill, the group or its individual members should not communicate with the recall or referral base about the group's collective or individual professional abilities. Of course, the practice staff or family may want to write to the patients and referral base to satisfy expectations for continued care.

• *Address Specialty Practice Issues*
Specialty groups should be prepared to consider the possibility of more travel time for the assisting members and the preservation of the practice goodwill territory. Mutual-assistance groups are invaluable in facilitating the initiation of the transition process, while the family is addressing other crisis issues.

Disability Insurance

The clinical ability and license to deliver dental care is a dentist's most valuable asset. Therefore, one of the most important financial decisions a dentist can make is to select appropriate disability insurance to protect that asset and the income from which it flows. There is a 30% chance that a 35-year-old dentist will become disabled for more than 90 days during his or her lifetime. A 35-year-old dentist earning $150,000 annually is estimated to generate $5.5 million by age 60, assuming a 3% inflation rate. That is an enormous amount of earning power to protect from disability.

If a practice owner cannot afford personal disability insurance, it is critical for him or her to buy overhead disability insurance for the practice. This insurance covers the salaries and payroll taxes of the owner and the staff, as well as the rent or mortgage payment and other basic operating expenses of the practice. A bare minimum policy is inexpensive, but usually is limited to a two-year coverage period.

What to Look for in a Disability Insurance Policy

Elements to help a dentist determine adequate personal disability protection include the following.

How Much Coverage Is Needed?

Coverage sufficient to replace at least 60% of personal earnings should be purchased, assuming that the disability income is not taxable. Prepare an analysis of personal income needs, taking into consideration current living expenses as well as future needs, such as education financing, to confirm that coverage is sufficient. Whether or not the disability benefits are taxable will depend on whether or not the premiums are paid with after-tax dollars or written off as a practice expense. Paying the premiums with after-tax dollars ensures that the disability benefits are not taxed.

Does the Policy Have an "Own Occupation" Clause?

"Own occupation" coverage is the best that can be purchased because the disability benefits are paid if the dentist is unable to perform the usual and substantial duties of dentistry, even if he or she chooses to work in another occupation. Other lesser levels of coverage are for "regular occupation," which pays the benefits while the dentist is unemployed but ceases to pay if he or she chooses to work in another occupation, and "any occupation," which basically states that if the dentist qualifies to work at any job (including as a greeter at Wal-Mart), the insurance company is off the hook.

How Long Is the Waiting Period for the Payment of Benefits?

All disability policies define a waiting or elimination period, which is the amount of time that elapses before payments start. During this waiting period, which ranges from 30 to 180 days, the dentist is expected to provide self-insurance. Premiums decrease drastically if the dentist chooses a waiting period of 90 days rather than 30 days.

Is the Policy Non-Cancellable?

This provision means that the insurance company must continue to provide coverage and premiums can't be increased as long as premiums are paid.

What Is the Maximum Benefit Payment Term?

All policies have a length of time during which they will continue paying monthly benefits (two years, 10 years, to age 65, or lifetime). Most dentists should choose the "age 65" option.

Does the Policy Offer Partial or Residual Benefits?

This is an important feature to look for. If a dentist cannot carry on his or her job full time, but can work part time, then the insurance company will pay benefits equal to the drop in personal income.

Many policies require a drop of 20% in personal income and a continuous disability of at least 30 days before the insured is eligible for residual benefits.

Are There COLA and FIO Options?

The cost of living adjustment (COLA) clause will provide increased benefits in the event of a very long disability. Its purpose is to protect the purchasing power of the disability income. The future income option (FIO) clause will allow for increases in coverage as the dentist's income increases, without having to provide evidence of insurability. This rider is important for young dentists, who are initially unable to receive the level of coverage they will require in the future because of insufficient current practice income.

Was All Medical History Disclosed at the Time of Application for Coverage?

The insurance company will not hire investigators to verify all the details of the application. However, applicants should make sure to disclose all ailments and illnesses, as to do otherwise is to risk being declined for coverage or losing coverage in the future if the insurance company determines that all was not disclosed at the time of application.

CHAPTER 13

Hot Topics

Marketing Your Dental Practice

Many dentists think their fees stop people from going ahead with treatment. They believe this because those patients who balk at moving forward very often say it's the fee that is the problem. However, in truth consumers want and will pay for value. Cost is rarely a barrier for a committed consumer.

The majority of patients and prospective patients view the clinical skill of their dentist as having a great deal of value and, if committed to pursuing the care recommended, will not quibble over price. However, many of these same patients and prospective patients, if not committed to pursuing the care recommended, will very likely use the price of the care as a cover.

Dentists are making a huge mistake when they use price to sell services. What should be developed and sold is the value offered rather than positioning the practice as the lowest bidder in the market. Leading with price as your value statement reduces your ability to successfully offer (sell) higher-level dental value, which might include comprehensive restorative dentistry. If you are only doing one-tooth-at-a-time dentistry, the reason to build value might be lessened somewhat. However, if you want to provide "future benefits" from your expertise, which requires a large value investment by the consumer, why start them on the path of expecting it for less?

Value building takes into account that everyone has certain areas of their life where they will spend more or less than their circumstance might imply they can. When people perceive higher value, they will sacrifice a lot to get it. It is why people buy $50,000 SUVs, even though they are single, make just enough to pay all their bills, live where there is no snow, and do no off-road driving. They are buying perceived value! It is not always logical, but it is what consumers do. Therefore, this is not about income, cost or status — it is about where each person perceives value. It is also about how you as dentists present and "teach" value. This is not to say that people should pay more — but that they should know the real value of your dental brand.

The basic marketing strategy of consistency, frequency and volume is a very powerful arsenal.

Building your marketing program on a foundation comprised of these three general concepts can create the type of activity you need and want.

No one changes their mind or moves off the dime without a consistent value argument. Communicating with consistency is the only way to make a noticeable dent in this reality. If you are not consistently communicating your value proposition, the consumer's perception of their need for the value of your services will diminish. Frequency in marketing gets consumers to act. Without frequent encounters with your value proposition, consumers will not show up at your office and pursue recommended treatment. Volume for a dental practice means approaching enough people to improve the odds you are talking to those who are ready to pay for your services. Yellow Page books and the Internet are relatively passive modes of volume marketing. An example of a more proactive mode of volume marketing is mailers. If 10,000 mailers are sent out and 0.5% of the recipients are persuaded to seek out your services, the result is 50 new patients.

The Paperless Office

The paperless office — promised since the first desktop computers started appearing in the 1980s — has yet to become a reality for most companies. Despite the increasing use of computers in all types of businesses, a good portion of most day-to-day work is still paper-based.

When we think of a paperless office, we envision an efficient way of conducting business — something that is not compromising on quality and saves time and effort on our part and puts all office documents at our fingertips. If you are considering moving from paper to electronic files, but aren't sure where to start, here are a few suggestions:

- First, make the commitment to the process of moving toward the paperless goal. The key is dedication and a well-organized approach.

- Second, ensure your hardware is up to the demands of the increased amount of scanning, processing and storage. Dual monitors are very helpful in simultaneously scanning, storing and dead-lining. Network servers need the ability to store 1 to 5 GB per dentist per year. Having a reliable backup system and testing it often is critical.

- Third, plan and test. Spending months of planning and isolated testing of systems and procedures avoids having to start over and over.

A truly paperless office is never going to happen. No matter how diligently you try to reduce or even eliminate the paper you generate, others will still send you paper for years to come. Even so, you can become paperLESS and much more efficient in your practice. Employing a creative and common sense approach to scanning, and leveraging anti-paper PDF tools, you can transform your desktop landscape. Once you go paperLESS, you will find that piles shrink. You will touch the paper less, chase around the office for the paper less, and you'll find more profits, more enjoyment and better client responsiveness in your practice.

To Catch a Thief

The Association of Certified Fraud Examiners estimated that in 2003 alone, embezzlement cost American businesses $660 billion, or 6% of total revenues. And while big companies get the big headlines, the small businesses are the ones taking the big losses. There are, unfortunately, many trusted employees pilfering from small businesses. In fact, a study conducted by the U.S. Department of Commerce found that about one-third of all employees steal from their employers.

In general, most dental practice owners believe that their employees, particularly long-term employees, are inherently honest and can be trusted. Consequently, few dentists place adequate checks and balances upon the business of their practices.

The following are some signs you can watch for that have been observed as indicators that employee theft may be occurring within the practice:

1. Behavior Patterns

The perpetrator will often display several behavior patterns, that if viewed in combination, can be a strong indicator of fraud.

- The employee is always the first to arrive at work and the last to leave.

- The employee never takes vacation unless the entire office is closed or will only take a couple of days.

- The employee rarely, if ever, takes sick days or personal days off.

- The employee refuses to teach other employees his or her job, claiming that others will mess up the "system," or that he or she does things just so, etc.

- The employee adamantly opposes any changes to the accounting system.

- The employee has an unusually high standard of living considering his or her salary.

- The employee provides unreasonable explanations and/or becomes annoyed in response to questions regarding their work process, activities, habits, etc.

- The employee is highly critical of others.

2. Complaints

Frequently, your practice will receive tips or complaints, which indicate a fraudulent action is going on. Even if the motives of the complainant are suspect, the allegations usually have merit and warrant investigation.

3. Stale and Increasing Items in Deposit Account Reconciliations

In bank reconciliations, deposits or checks not included in the reconciliation could include evidence of deposits and checks fraudulently diverting funds to an employee. Because unreconciled items are frequently not removed from reconciliation reports, the number of items will tend to steadily increase where a fraudulent scheme is under way.

4. Excessive Voids

Voided patient receipts could mean that the patient paid, the payment was diverted to the use of the perpetrator, and the internal copies of the receipt were voided to cover the theft.

5. Excessive Credit Memos

Similar to excessive voids, this technique can be used to cover the theft of cash. A credit memo to a phony customer is written out, and the cash is taken to keep the cash account in balance.

6. Common Names and Addresses for Refunds

This fraud often involves insurance refunds received by the practice in error which are subsequently directed to a nonexistent customer at an address (typically a PO Box, friend or family member) controlled by the perpetrator.

7. General Ledger Out-of-Balance

When funds, inventory or assets are stolen and not covered by a fictitious entry, the general ledger will be out of balance.

8. Adjustment to Receivables or Payables

In cases where patient payments are misappropriated, adjustments to receivables are usually made by the perpetrator to cover the shortages. Perpetrators use adjustments to trade payables to prop up a phony billing scheme designed to convert cash to his or her own use.

9. Write-Off of Receivables

Comparing the write-off of receivables by patients or insurance companies may lead to information indicating that the employee has absconded with patient payments. Only the doctor should have the authority to write off an account.

10. Slow Collections

If a patient or insurance company that has always paid within guidelines has a past due balance, it may indicate the misappropriation of a payment received.

11. Excessive Purchases

Excessive purchases can be an indicator of scams involving fictitious payees and collusion between an employee and suppliers rep. An investigation of excessive purchasing may also lead to the discovery of phantom vendors where the payments for goods or services go to an address controlled by the perpetrator.

12. Duplicate Payments

Duplicate payments are sometimes converted to the use of an employee. The employee may notice the duplicate payment, then he or she may prepare a phony endorsement of the check or turn it into cash at the bank.

13. Employee Overtime

Employees being paid for overtime hours not worked by altering time sheets before or after your approval (if required) is another red flag.

14. Inventory and Supply Shortages

Normal shrinkage over a period of time can be computed through historical analysis. Excessive shrinkage could explain a host of fraudulent activity, from embezzlement to theft of inventory or phantom inventory.

15. Charge Accounts and Credit Cards

The perpetrator makes charges for his or her own benefit to the practice's charge accounts and credit cards. When the bill comes in, it is paid in the normal course, and the merchandise is used by the employee.

The following steps will go a long way toward protecting you and your practice from financial fraud.

- Review deposit tickets on a regular basis. The average amount of cash in a practice is 2% to 5% of revenues, but whatever the amount, it should not vary significantly from month to month.

- Do not depend on just one person to handle the practice accounting. Insist on cross-training staff to work at the front desk.

- Establish a system in which all employees who use the computer must log on with personal identification codes.

- Remember, embezzlers love the hands-off dentist because they know he or she is never looking over their shoulders. Learn how to access key reports, and restrict access to certain reports such as the Audit Trail and other production/collection reports that the staff does not need on a regular basis.

- Review all invoices and sign all checks. Make sure there is an invoice for every check written.

- Do not have a signature stamp for signing checks unless it is kept under lock and key and only you have access to it.

- Keep the practice checkbook under lock and key until the bookkeeper needs it.

- Randomly conduct spot checks every few days, and compare the practice's schedule with the day sheet. Verify that all the treatment delivered was posted, and scan the adjustments to ensure there was a valid reason for making them.

- Carefully review the practice charge card statement(s) for suspicious activity.

- Compare bank deposit records with the day sheet and make bank deposits daily.

- Never allow the same person to prepare the bank deposit and take it to the bank.

- Have bank statements and canceled checks sent directly to your home.

- Ask questions and make sure all employees know that you are interested in and monitoring the accounting.

If you suspect an employee of engaging in questionable activity, you should take immediate action to verify or debunk that hunch. The suspicion should not be shared with anyone else in the practice.

Leasing Space for a Dental Practice

Signing a lease can be one of the most important actions a dentist will take as a practice and small business owner. Many dental tenants make the mistake of paying attention to only the occupancy cost and location. However, one of the most important purposes of a lease is allocating the responsibility and risks of loss that can occur to people or property.

Dental tenants often assume their landlord will provide certain services that end up not being provided. This is because if it's not in the lease, the landlord does not, and is not, likely to provide it. While the following list is not exhaustive, an office lease typically will:

- Stipulate that the landlord will regulate the temperature ranges to ensure comfort during business hours

- State that the landlord will ensure the property complies with applicable laws and will undertake maintenance and repair of the common lobby, hallway areas, and restrooms, as well as of the building structure and roof, building systems and utilities

- State that the landscaping, sidewalks, and parking areas will be well maintained and that the landlord will undertake snow and ice removal (if applicable)

- Stipulate whether running water will be provided by the landlord (and whether it will include hot water or whether the dentist will be obligated to purchase a water heater for the space)

- State that the landlord will furnish the space with reasonable amounts of electricity for the kinds of equipment the dentist intends to install

A lease should also address what happens if the building experiences a casualty such as theft, fire, flood or vandalism. The lease should state that the landlord is obligated to give notice after a casualty, stating the length of time needed to complete necessary repairs. Again, landlords are not required to provide any services beyond those that are clearly stated in the lease. Dental tenants therefore, should have an experienced real estate attorney review and/or negotiate the legal terms and conditions of the office lease.

Closing the Door

If closing a dental practice or discontinuing the practice of dentistry becomes necessary, the owner should review all of the local, state and federal laws — including the Health Insurance Portability and Accountability Act (HIPAA) — governing the discontinuance of a dental practice.

The tangible assets, such as dental and office equipment, may be sold to another dentist or a company that specializes in purchasing used equipment, or may be donated to a charitable organization. If it is donated to charity, all or part of it may not be tax-deductible (an accountant's guidance in this matter is needed).

As owner of the dental patient charts, the dentist has the responsibility to maintain the patient records for a period of time. A succeeding dentist-colleague in the area may be enticed to take over the responsibility of maintaining these charts. The benefit to the dentist taking over the patient charts would be gaining some additional patients and income. If the patient charts are transferred, great care should be taken to comply with local, state and federal laws, including HIPAA (consult the applicable state dental practice laws for direction). As an example, at the time of this writing, some of the requirements of the state of Indiana for dentists discontinuing a practice are as follows:

- Notify all active patients that the dentist intends to discontinue practice in the community, either in writing or by publication once a week for three consecutive weeks in a newspaper of general circulation in the community.

- Encourage patients to seek the services of another dentist.

- Make reasonable arrangements for the transfer of the dentist's records, or copies thereof, to the succeeding practitioner or, at the written request of the patient, to the patient.

Seven Important Methods for Protecting Your Assets

As doctors' wealth increases, their primary focus shifts from accumulating to protecting their hard-earned assets from the increasing perils of frivolous lawsuits. Unfortunately, increased business has also raised the odds of being targeted for a lawsuit. Furthermore, the restrictions placed by managed care on patient clinical care and reduced fees have resulted in a tremendous increase in medical malpractice litigation and bodes the same for participating dentists. Contractual disputes have also increased litigation between doctors and managed care plan companies. Finally, the declining fortunes of physician and dental publicly traded management companies promise increased litigation between those companies and affiliating doctors looking for an out.

Given these increasing threats of litigation, it's more important than ever for doctors to be forewarned and forearmed so as to protect their personal assets. Waiting until a lawsuit has been threatened or commenced is usually too late to protect the doctor's assets.

As part of McGill & Hill Group's comprehensive tax and financial planning service, they analyze the doctor's assets to consider ways to hold, transfer and invest in order to protect them from creditors' claims. Below are the several strategies they recommend to protect the doctor's assets from this growing threat:

1. Maintain Adequate Insurance Coverages

Proper insurance coverages are a second line of defense. Doctors should maintain adequate malpractice insurance coverage (generally $1 million to $3 million), adequate general liability coverage ($1 million) to protect against non-clinical practice risks, as well as adequate automobile and homeowner's insurance coverages. Finally, they recommend that doctors buy a $1 million umbrella liability insurance policy, providing additional coverage beyond automobile and homeowner's limits at a cost of only a few hundred dollars per year.

2. Operate as a Professional Corporation (PC)

Operating as a solo professional corporation will help protect the doctor's personal assets from corporate tax and other practice liabilities, excluding his or her own malpractice.

3. Transfer Assets into Spouse's Name

Transferring assets to the non-doctor spouse can be an effective way to "even-up" asset values between them, thereby assuring that each spouse can fully utilize the unified transfer tax exemption. These transfers can generally be accomplished without any gift tax paid during a lifetime and can provide substantial estate tax savings. However, doctors considering this strategy should have a stable marriage, and take action before there has been any non-renewal of liability insurance, or before a lawsuit has been threatened or commenced. If doctors shift assets to their spouse or another party after events have occurred that would give creditors an actual or potential claim, the transaction may be rescinded as a "fraudulent conveyance."

4. Use Joint Asset Ownership

Maintaining joint ownership of assets, particularly real estate held as tenants by the entirety, is an effective asset protection strategy in some states. While these assets are still subject to creditors who have a claim against both spouses, they are generally beyond the reach of a malpractice claim only against one spouse (the doctor). While it may be important to transfer assets into a single spouse's name to take advantage of the unified transfer tax exclusion referred to above, the remaining assets, especially real estate, should continue to be held jointly.

5. Establish a Family Limited Partnership (FLP) or Limited Liability Company (LLC)

Even when creditors threaten to sue, a transfer of assets to an FLP or LLC can be successful in minimizing the doctor's liability exposure. Under this approach, the doctor transfers assets into the limited partnership in exchange for general and limited partnership interests. As general partner, the doctor retains control and management over the assets owned by the partnership. As a general rule, creditors cannot reach assets within the partnership, nor can a limited partnership be dissolved due to a suit against an individual partner. Rather, an individual creditor is restricted to getting a "charging order" against the doctor's partnership interest. If the doctor's creditor attaches his interest, the creditor must pay tax on the income earned by the partnership interest whether or not it is distributed, and has no voice in management, no ownership interest and can receive income if and only to the extent it is distributed as permitted under the partnership agreement. This makes a family limited partnership interest particularly unappealing for attachment by a judgment creditor. In addition, all fraudulent conveyance problems are avoided since the doctor is receiving an asset of equal value (partnership interest) in exchange for the assets transferred into the partnership. The doctor is simply benefiting from the fact that the assets are being converted from a form which is easily reachable by creditors to one which is most difficult for creditors to attach and seize.

All jurisdictions have now enacted statutes permitting the formation of limited liability companies (LLCs). While being taxed similarly to family limited partnerships, limited liability companies offer one important advantage. While a general partner in the family limited partnership is subject to unlimited liability for claims made against the partnership (but not the doctor), all members holding ownership interests in a limited liability company are fully protected from liability. Accordingly, where the partnership engages in one or more hazardous activities, use of an LLC is generally preferable.

6.   Purchase Life Insurance or Annuity Contracts Naming the Spouse and Children as Beneficiaries

In many states, creditors cannot attach or have access to the cash surrender value of life insurance policies, or the proceeds of annuity contracts, provided they are not paid to the insured's probate estate. While these generally make poor investments, doctors in those states can protect substantial amounts from the claims of creditors by investing assets in these policies.

7. Irrevocable Trusts

Life insurance trusts are the most common form of irrevocable trusts used. Transferring assets into an irrevocable trust for the benefit of the doctor's spouse or children can be an effective estate protection strategy, provided the transfers are made while the doctor is solvent, and before any lawsuit is filed or threatened. In most cases, assets held by an irrevocable trust will not be subject to the claims of the doctor's creditors, nor will they be subject to the claims of the beneficiaries' creditors if the trust contains the standard spendthrift provisions.

Legal Structure & DBAs

Prospective business owners must select both a legal structure (business entity form) and a name (DBA) for their new business. You may want to consult with an attorney before choosing a legal structure, particularly if more than one person will own the business. You may also want to check with an accountant since your selection choice will affect the taxes you must pay and how you report them.

If you choose a name for the business other than your personal name, you will be creating an Assumed Business Name, also known as "Doing Business As" or DBA, and you will need to register that name with the Secretary of State's office. You may use an Assumed Business Name for any type of business entity.

Following are descriptions of the various legal structures (business entity forms) recognized in most states.

A Sole Proprietorship is the simplest business structure to organize, so many new businesses start this way. All businesses are considered sole proprietorships unless the owner specifically registers the business with the Secretary of State's office as a corporation, partnership, LLC, or non-profit entity. A sole proprietorship is owned by one individual (a husband and wife cannot own a sole proprietorship) who has complete control of the business and is responsible for all business decisions and financial obligations. Business revenue is considered personal income of the owner and is taxed at the owner's personal tax rate. All liabilities created by the business are the personal liabilities of the owner.

A sole proprietorship that uses a name other than that of the individual owner must file a "Certificate of Assumed Business Name" with the Secretary of State's office. You do not need to file any additional paper work with the Secretary of State other than your certificate of Assumed Business Name.

A business organized as a sole proprietorship terminates upon the death or bankruptcy of the business owner. The property used in the business is disposed of according to the terms of the owner's will or a court order, since it is considered the owner's personal property. It is often more difficult to sell a sole proprietorship than another form of business because the law does not recognize a sole proprietorship as a separate legal entity apart from the owner.

A Partnership involves two or more people (including married couples) who are conducting a business together. This business structure is fairly simple to establish, but may have more costs than a sole proprietorship because each partner must file a separate tax return.

Each partner has the power to act on behalf of the business, including financial matters, and to legally bind the other partner(s). This can create a potentially dangerous situation if all partners are not informed and agree on issues. Therefore, it is strongly recommended that an attorney prepare a written partnership agreement to govern the business. The agreement establishes the rules by which the partners will conduct business. This should include the responsibilities and authority of each partner and how the business decisions, including financial decisions, will be made. The agreement should also contain an exit plan should one partner wish to leave the business.

Partners share in the profits and losses of the business according to the terms of the partnership agreement, and profits are taxed as personal income. While a partnership is recognized as a separate legal entity from the individual partners, the partners' personal assets may be used to satisfy the business's creditors, including debts incurred for the business by only one partner.

Unless a legal partnership agreement has been created, partnerships end with the death, retirement, expulsion, incapacity or personal bankruptcy of one of the partners.

Partnerships must file a "Certificate of Assumed Business Name" with the Secretary of State's office if they do not operate under the legal names of all partners.

A Limited Partnership is made up of two or more individuals who jointly own a business. This partnership form allows for both general and limited partners. Limited partners are generally financially liable for debts only to the extent of their investment in the business. They have limited or no control over management of the company. The general partners manage the company and face the greatest potential risk and reward from the business operations.

A Corporation can be complex and expensive to organize. Legal assistance is strongly advised because originals of the corporation's Articles of Incorporation must be filed with the Secretary of State's office and the corporation must create and adopt bylaws to address the management and regulation of the corporation's affairs.

A corporation is a separate legal entity from its owners. It may be privately or publicly held. The corporation is controlled by its Board of Directors, which is, in turn, controlled by the owners (shareholders) of the corporation. Most corporate profits are taxed twice — once as income to the corporation and once as a dividend to the owners (shareholders). Corporations must hold annual meetings, keep minutes of meetings and file reports of their activities. Corporations are dissolved by a vote of the shareholders or by court order.

There are several types of corporations including C, S, and Professional Service Corporations.

- A C Corporation is the original form of a corporation. The corporation files its own income tax returns and owners (shareholders) are taxed only if dividends are paid to them.

- An S Corporation offers the protection of a corporation with the flexibility of a partnership. Profits and losses pass through to the owners as if the business were a partnership. The corporation must file Articles of Incorporation, adopt bylaws and hold regular meetings. An S Corp. cannot be owned by more than 75 individuals and cannot be owned by another corporation, partnership or a non-U.S. resident. An S Corp. cannot issue stock.

- A Professional Service Corporation consists of individuals engaged in a limited number of professions, such as medical, dental, legal, landscape architects, architects or veterinarians.

A Limited Liability Company (LLC) provides the liability protection of a corporation and the federal tax benefits of a partnership or sole proprietorship. An LLC is formed in a manner similar to a corporation. The name of the company must include the words "Limited Company," "LLC," or "Limited Liability Company." In an LLC, the individual members or managers are not personally liable for debts, obligations or liabilities of the company. Even a one-person LLC should have a legal Operating Agreement prepared by an attorney.

A Professional Limited Liability Company (PLLC) is an LLC whose members offer a professional service, such as legal, medical or dental services. The name of the company must include the words "Professional Limited Company," "PLLC," or "Professional Limited Liability Company."

Managing Contributor

K.M. "Mac" Winston, CFP

PPC LOAN
9303 New Trails Drive, Suite 375, The Woodlands, TX 77381
Phone: (281) 419-0400 | *mac@ppcloan.com*
www.ppcloan.com

Mac Winston is president and chief lending officer for PPC LOAN, one of the nation's leading sources of bank financing for dentists, veterinarians and Allstate agents since 1998. He has over 30 years of banking experience and has specialized in lending to dentists, veterinarians, accountants, insurance agents, and other service sector professionals since 1992. In addition to having served as a member of the Practice Management Faculty of the Northwestern Dental School, Mr. Winston has also participated in the University of Texas, San Antonio, and the University of Las Vegas Dental Schools' practice management curriculums. He has published numerous articles in *Dental Economics Magazine* and other prominent dental publications. He graduated from Southern Methodist University with a B.B.A. in accounting and is a Certified Financial Planner.

Contributors

Peter Ackerman, CPA

ADS Midwest - Chicago
195 North Harbor Drive, Suite 202, Chicago, IL 60601
Phone: (888) 416-5728 x312 | *petera@adstransitions.com*
www.ADStransitions.com

Peter J. Ackerman is the principal of the Chicago office of American Dental Sales (ADS) Midwest. Mr. Ackerman is a graduate of Miami University in Oxford, Ohio, with degrees in accounting, general business and finance. He began his career in private accounting at Lane Industries, Northbrook, Ill., a holding company over numerous organizations including General Binding Company, Lane Hotels, Lane Aviation, Secret Communication and several other subsidiaries. In 1996, after earning his Certified Public Accountant designation, Mr. Ackerman became a principal in ADS. He has served on the dental student liaison committee, as a director, vice president and president of ADS.

Mr. Ackerman currently serves as director of Professional Management Consultants Association, an association of over 300 dental and medical consultants educating professionals on risk management, as well as providing professional liability insurance to its members. He is a licensed real estate broker in Illinois and Wisconsin, a licensed business broker and a member of Practice Valuation Study Group. Each year Mr. Ackerman lectures to dental audiences, residency classes, dental district meetings, continuing education courses and other dental society functions throughout the Midwest and United States.

Bill E. Avery, DDS

Professional Practice Sales & Appraisals, Inc.
9420 Layton Ct. NE, Albuquerque, NM 87111
Phone: (888) 416-5728 x505 | *billa@adstransitions.com*
www.ADStransitions.com

Dr. Bill Avery has been valuing and selling dental practices in New Mexico since 1993. Dr. Avery graduated from Baylor College of Dentistry and completed specialized training in periodontics and obtained a Ph.D. in electron microscopy at Baylor. After active duty in the U.S. Navy, he began the private practice of periodontics in 1973. Dr. Avery operates under the premise that a transaction must be fair and equitable to both seller and purchaser in order for the transaction to be labeled a success. He is a member of the ADA, NMDA, and the Institute of Business Appraisers.

Roy Berry

Roy Berry Consultants
(317) 436-8321 | *RoyBerry@RoyBerry.com*

Dr. Charles Blair

Dr. Charles Blair & Associates, Inc.
547 Highland Street, Mount Holly, NC 28120
Phone: (704) 827-6295
Toll Free: (866) 858-7596 | *info@drcharlesblair.com*

Dr. Charles Blair is a contributing editor for *Dental Economics Magazine,* and a former practicing dentist who now provides consulting services to the dental industry on a full-time basis. His business, Dr. Charles Blair & Associates, Inc., near Charlotte, N.C., specializes in providing highly effective, customized consultations to individual doctors and staff who want to maximize practice profitability and personal income through sound, proven business strategies.

A graduate of Erskine College, Dr. Blair earned his Doctorate at the University of North Carolina at Chapel Hill. He also holds degrees in accounting, business administration, mathematics and dental surgery. A widely-read and highly-respected author, Dr. Blair has written the E-Z Tax Cookbook; co-authored "Marketing for the Dental Practice," "Employing Family Members in Your Practice: A Tax Bonanza!," and recently published "Coding with Confidence: The 'Go To' Guide for CDT-2007/2008." In addition, he has published numerous articles in dental magazines, and is an acclaimed speaker for national, state and local dental groups, study clubs, and professional organizations. He offers leading-edge presentations in the business/finance/and dental insurance arena of dentistry.

Frank J. Brown, JD, LLM

ADS Watson, Brown & Associates, Inc.

1202 Richardson Drive, Suite #203, Richardson, TX 75080

Phone: (888) 416-5728 x972 | *frankb@adstransitions.com*

www.ADStransitions.com

Frank J. Brown graduated from Southern Methodist University School of Law with a master of laws in taxation. He completed his business degree from Arizona State University and his law degree from the University of Arkansas. As a tax attorney he began his professional career in the tax department at Peat, Marwick, Mitchell & Company, one of the big eight international accounting firms. Brown's accounting background provides a broad exposure to tax, accounting and business matters.

Mr. Brown entered private law practice and handled his first dental practice transition in the late 1980s. Brown entered the private business sector and was involved in the transportation, insurance, finance and medical supply distribution industries. Brown joined the firm of Watson and Associates in 2004.

Mr. Brown has contributed articles to major dental publications, such as *Dental Economics Magazine* and *Dental Entrepreneur.* He is a frequent speaker at the Texas Dental Association's annual event, the Southwest Dental Conference, Houston's Star of the South Dental Meeting, and Baylor College of Dentistry. He currently serves as the president of ADS, a national association of dental practice transition specialists. He has also served as the director of the J. Rueben Clark Law Society Dallas/Fort Worth and director of the B.Y.U. Management Society Dallas/Fort Worth. Brown is a licensed attorney in Texas and Arizona.

Watson, Brown & Associates provides practice appraisals, pre-planning for contingencies, partnership arrangements, brokerage and sales, associate arrangements, and purchaser representation services with a common sense, bottom line approach for dentists.

John M. Cahill, MBA

Contact - Tim Giroux, DDS
Western Practice Sales / John M. Cahill and Associates
437 Century Park Drive, Suite A, Yuba City, CA 95991
Phone: (888) 416-5728 x530 | *timg@adstransitions.com*
www.ADStransitions.com

John M. Cahill is nationally known as one the country's premier transition specialists. Western Practice Sales / John M. Cahill Associates has provided quality brokerage services to healthcare professionals for more than 20 years, and is the only brokerage firm that represents sellers and locates buyers throughout California, Arizona, and Nevada from one central office. A member of American Dental Sales (ADS), a regular contributor to *Dental Economics Magazine* and a frequent featured speaker for many dental groups over the years, he brings knowledge, experience and integrity to the transition process with more than 35 years of experience in the dental industry.

Dr. Tim Giroux established his own dental practice in Scottsdale, Ariz., upon graduation from Creighton University, School of Dentistry in 1983. He relocated to Northern California upon selling his highly successful practice after 15 years, Dr. Giroux brings a unique perspective and personal experience in dental associateships, practice start-up, sales, and workback situations to serve and assist practice owners during their business transitions.

Alan Clemens

The Clemens Group
104 E. 40th Street, Suite # 503, New York, NY 10016
Phone: (888) 416-5728 x816 | *alanc@adstransitions.com*
www.ADStransitions.com

The Clemens Group are dental practice brokers serving the New York/New Jersey area for over 25 years. As transition specialists who deal exclusively with the dental profession, The Clemens Group has unique capabilities to analyze and evaluate dentists' particular circumstances and come up with creative solutions to meet their needs and expectations.

Randy M. Daigler

DBS Professional Practice Brokers
PO Box 280, 6006 Westside Saginaw Road, Bay City, MI 48707
Phone: (888) 416-5728 x989 | *randyd@adstransitions.com*
www.ADStransitions.com

Randy Marie Daigler is transition manager for DBS Professional Practice Brokers, founded by Theodore C. Schumann, CPA, CBC, CFP. DBS Professional Practice Brokers provides dentists in Michigan with a variety of services including assistance in buying or selling a practice, associate recruitment, associate buy-in/out, partner searches, practice mergers, facilitating space-sharing arrangements, and facilitating the formation of Mutual Aid Groups. Ms. Daigler is a graduate of the University of Detroit. She is a guest lecturer at both the University of Michigan Dental School and University of Detroit Mercy School of Dentistry. She presents to local study clubs and society meetings as well at national continuing education programs on topics ranging from transition to death & disability, as well as buyer representation. Ms. Daigler is on the executive committee of American Dental Sales (ADS).

Earl M. Douglas, DDS, MBA, BVAL

ADS South
11285 Elkins Road, Suite A2, Roswell, GA 30076
Phone: (888) 416-5728 x770 | *adssouth@adstransitions.com*
www.ADStransitions.com

Dr. Earl M. Douglas is the founder and president of Professional Practice Consultants, Ltd. Dr. Douglas earned his Doctor of Dental Surgery degree from the Baltimore College of Dental Surgery, Dental School, University of Maryland in 1971. He practiced in the U.S. Army Dental Corps at Fort Benning, Ga., from 1971 to 1974 and in Stuttgart, West Germany, from 1974 to 1977. Dr. Douglas was in private practice in Atlanta from 1978 through 1982. After the sale of his private practice, he began his career in practice transition consulting. He received his Master in Business Administration degree from Brenau College in 1984 and founded Professional Practice Consultants, Ltd. Dr. Douglas founded American Dental Sales (ADS) in 1996 and served as its first president. He is the author of cash flow analysis software used by professional brokers and lenders. Dr. Douglas was awarded the Business Valuator Accredited in Litigation (BVAL) designation from The Institute of Business Appraisers in 2007. He is also a contributing author for *Dental Economics Magazine* and has presented numerous seminars for *Dental Economics* and state dental associations. Dr. Douglas is a member of the Practice Valuation Study Group and The Institute of Business Appraisers.

Bob Fitzgerald, CPA
McCormick and Fitzgerald Dental Practice Transitions
Retired

Guy Jaffe
ADS Midwest
2518 Bopp Road, St. Louis, MO 63131
Phone: (888) 416-5728 x314 | *guyj@adstransitions.com*
www.ADStransitions.com

Guy Jaffe is the principal of ADS Midwest (formerly The Dental Marketplace) in St. Louis, Mo. Mr. Jaffe has been appraising and selling dental practices exclusively since 1987. Previously, he was head of his own commercial real estate development and management firm and has served as director of Community and Economic Development for the state of Missouri. Mr. Jaffe is a member of Practice Valuation Study Group, a national organization dedicated to improving professional practice valuations, and a director of Metropolitan Capital Bank in Chicago. He is past president of American Dental Sales (ADS), the largest network of dental practice brokers in the United States. ADS Midwest serves members of the dental profession in Missouri, Illinois, Iowa and Wisconsin by providing practice valuations, practice sales, partnership formations, associate buy-ins and practice management consulting services.

Jim Kasper
Contact – Sarah K. Lynch
Jim Kasper Associates, LLC
PO Box 369, Keene, NH 03431
Phone: (888) 416-5728 x603 | *sarahl@adstransitions.com*
www.ADStransitions.com

Sarah K. Lynch is a partner in Jim Kasper Associates, LLC, a regional practice brokerage and transition firm serving dentists in New England and New York State since 1981, specializing in appraisals and sales of dental practices. Ms. Lynch has 13 years of practice brokerage and appraisal experience, completing over 900 practice transitions and 750 appraisals of both general and specialty practices. She lectures nationally on practice transitions and is a frequent guest speaker for several state and local dental associations, societies and dental practice related industries.

Gretchen O. Lovelace, MS, CFP, CPM

ADS Lovelace and Associates, Inc.
8202 Kelwood Avenue, Baton Rouge, LA 70806
Phone: (888) 416-5728 x225 | *adslovelace@adstransitions.com*
www.ADStransitions.com

Gretchen Ohlmeyer Lovelace is the president and founder of ADS Lovelace and Associates, Inc. Gretchen taught at the University of New Orleans, and conducted research in the Microbiology department at Louisiana State University School of Dentistry before returning to Baton Rouge and obtaining certifications in Financial Planning and Practice Management. She has 29 years of practice management experience and has been a guest lecturer at the LSU Dental School for the past 19 years, as well as at national, state, and local meetings. She is a member of The Financial Planning Association and the Institute of Business Appraisers, and is a realtor, and a notary. Practical, ethical, and professional practice promotion and practice transitions are Gretchen's main interests.

Robert J. Mallin, DS

PPC of NJ, Inc.
Retired

Gene McCormick, DDS

McCormick and Fitzgerald Dental Practice Transitions
Retired

John F. McDonnell

ADS McNor Group
1301 York Road, Suite 109, Lutherville, MD 21093
Phone: (888) 416-5728 x410 | *johnfm@adstransitions.com*
www.ADStransitions.com

John F. McDonnell has been working with the dental profession for over 40 years. He is the founder and president of ADS McNor Group, a dental brokerage and transition firm serving sellers and new owners. Mr.

McDonnell currently serves as a partner and principal of ADS McNor Group, which specializes in nationwide practice transitions, including sales, mergers and partnerships. He is a member and past president of American Dental Sales (ADS), representing the Mid-Atlantic region. He is widely published in dental periodicals, particularly *Dental Economics Magazine,* where his articles have appeared on a regular basis. He is a recognized speaker and lecturer on the topic of dental practice transitions.

Evan Myers

EMA Dental Practice Sales
Retired
Contact - Steve Wolff, DDS
(888) 416-5728 x816
steve@adstransitions.com

Karen Norris, CPA

ADS McNor Group
1301 York Road, Suite 109, Lutherville, MD 21093
Phone: (888) 416-5728 x410 | *johnfm@adstransitions.com*
www.ADStransitions.com

Karen Norris is a partner and principal and serves as chief executive officer of ADS McNor Group, which specializes in nationwide practice transitions, including sales, mergers partnerships, accounting, tax and financial planning, and practice optimization. She provides consultative leadership on projects for clients involving cash flow and profitability analyses, and the formulation of financial modeling. Ms. Norris has been serving the dental industry in the Mid-Atlantic region for over 18 years. As a certified public accountant, she has focused on the unique needs of dental practices and dental professionals relative to accounting and tax planning, and as a Certified Valuation Analyst (CVA), she has been recognized as an expert in the complex process of business valuation. She has focused this expertise on the dental practice and is recognized as one of the foremost valuators of dental practices both regionally and nationally.

Gary Schaub

ADS Oregon
PO Box 69155, Portland, OR 97239
Phone: (888) 416-5728 x503 | *garys@adstransitions.com*
www.ADStransitions.com

HELP Appraisals & Sales, Inc. appraises and sells dental and medical practices, with services including practice appraisals, practice sales, associate arrangements, associate/buy-in arrangements, and practice mergers. Mr. Schaub has personally appraised more than 1,500 health care practices and has been involved in the sale of over 400 practices since 1984. His background includes a B.S. in electrical engineering, a Master of Business Administration, and over 20 years of health care practice appraisal, sale, and transition experience. Mr. Schaub is a member of the Institute of Business Appraisers and chairman of the national Practice Valuation Study Group. He provides seminars and lectures for national dental societies, and has given four Table Clinic presentations at American Dental Association (ADA) meetings.

Ted Schumann, CPA, CBC, CFP, DBS

DBS Professional Practice Brokers
PO Box 280, 6006 Westside Saginaw Road, Bay City, MI 48707
Phone: (888) 416-5728 x989 | *teds@adstransitions.com*
www.ADStransitions.com

Ted Schumann began working with dentists in 1979 and formed Dental Business Services in 1983 for the primary purpose of helping dentists reach their personal and financial objectives. DBS Professional Practice Brokers, founded by Theodore C. Schumann, CPA, CBC, CFP, provides dentists in Michigan with a variety of services, including assistance in buying or selling a practice, associate recruitment, associate buy-in/out, partner searches, practice mergers, facilitating space-sharing arrangements, and facilitating the formation of Mutual Aid Groups. As president of DBS Professional Practice Brokers, Mr. Schumann consults with dentists on accounting, tax and financial planning, and practice management.

Mr. Schumann has been a guest lecturer at the University of Michigan Dental School and an adjunct professor at University of Detroit Mercy School of Dentistry. He has been sponsored for several years by the MDA as a speaker to senior practitioners. *Dental Economics Magazine* has sponsored Mr. Schumann to speak nationally for two years. He has written for *Dental Graduate, The New Doc – the MDA E-Zine for New Dentists*, and a monthly transitions column in *Dental Economics Magazine*. He is also Michigan's only member of the Academy of Dental CPAs, and a founding member and a past president of American Dental Sales (ADS), the nation's most respected practice broker organization.

Rich Seims, DDS
ADS Northwest
16300 Christensen Road, #213, Seattle, WA 98188
Phone: (888) 416-5728 x206 | *adsnorthwest@adstransitions.com*
www.ADStransitions.com

After practicing dentistry for 30 years, Dr. Rich Seims co-founded Consani Seims, Ltd., specializing in dental practice mergers and acquisitions. Consani Seims, Ltd. provides brokerage services for dental practices in Washington, Oregon, Montana, Idaho, Hawaii and Alaska. Dr. Seims is a senior broker/consultant and practice appraiser and is recognized as a seasoned facilitator and discreet confidante. He is a member of two nationally recognized dental practice transition organizations; The Practice Valuation Study Group and American Dental Sales (ADS), both acknowledged as leaders in the field of dental practice valuations and brokerage.

Kevin A. Shea, JD
Shea Practice Transitions, PA
6750 France Avenue South, Suite 114, Edina, MN 55435
Phone: (888) 416-5728 x952 | *kevins@adstransitions.com*
www.ADStransitions.com

Kevin A. Shea and Shea Practice Transitions are the foremost appraisers and brokers of dental practices in the upper Midwest. Shea Practice Transitions covers the states of Minnesota, North Dakota, South Dakota, as well as Northern Iowa and Western Wisconsin. Mr. Shea is an honors graduate from the University of St. Thomas and a Minnesota attorney. Since 1985, Shea Practice Transitions has brokered dental practice sales, designed and implemented numerous practice buy-ins and buyouts, as well as represented buyers with practice acquisitions. Mr. Shea has hundreds of hours of continuing education in business formations, appraisals, purchase agreements, estate planning and taxation. His expertise in this area is widely known and recommended throughout the upper Midwest. As one of his colleagues stated, "...Kevin has one of the brightest minds in the country when it comes to practice transitions."

Tom Smeed

Healthcare Practice Management, Inc.
Mark 1 Plaza Offices - Suite D
9948 West 87th Street, Overland Park, KS, 66212-4744
Phone: (888) 416-5728 x913 | *toms@adstransitions.com*
www.ADStransitions.com

Tom Smeed is founder and owner of Healthcare Practice Management, Inc., and past president and member of American Dental Sales (ADS), a nationwide, full-service brokering and consulting firm specializing in practice sales, appraisals and practice transition services. Healthcare Practice Management, Inc. provides the business management skills, procedures, training and counseling that augment dentists' professional skills. Mr. Smeed is a graduate of the University of Minnesota with a degree in business. For 20 years, he worked for one of the largest dental suppliers, 14 years as manager of one of its multimillion dollar offices. Mr. Smeed presently works with more than 100 professional offices in a 16-state area and has had clients in Australia. For the past 22 years, as owner of Healthcare Practice Management, Inc., he has helped professionals define and reach their goals in an effort to improve their quality of life. He helps doctors start and develop outstanding practices; buy, sell and transition their practices; set up associateship arrangements; and counsels them on their personal and career opportunities. As a member of ADS, Mr. Smeed appraises and sells dental practices in the states of Kansas, Missouri, Iowa, and Nebraska. He has lectured in the United States and Australia on Practice Management, Staff Management, Self Management, Patient Management, Practice Sales and Practice Transition and contributed articles that appeared in a national dental publication. He also is a member of the Practice Valuation Study Group.

H. M. (Hy) Smith, MBA

ADS Florida, LLC / Professional Transitions, Inc.
Contact: Paul Rang
999 Vanderbilt Beach Road, Suite 200, Naples, FL 34108
Phone: (888) 416-5728 x239 | *adsflorida@adstransitions.com*
www.ADStransitions.com

H.M. (Hy) Smith is president and founder of ADS Florida, a practice brokerage and consulting firm. Mr. Smith has been involved in dentistry for over 30 years and is currently the director of transition strategies at the Pride Institute. He has lectured at the University of Florida, Nova Southeastern University and presents a practice management course on transition strategies to the University of the Pacific, Marquette, and Indiana University dental schools. Mr. Smith has presented to the American College of Prosthodontists, the Greater New York Dental Meeting, Pankey Institute, the Florida National Dental Congress, as well as numerous local dental societies. He is a member of the Practice Valuation Study Group and a member of the Institute of Business Appraisers. Mr. Smith has also written numerous articles for *Dental Economics Magazine* on transition subjects and issues.

Terry D. Watson, DDS

ADS Watson, Brown & Associates
1202 Richardson Drive, Suite #203, Richardson, TX 75080
Phone: (888) 416-5728 x972 | *adswba@adstransitions.com*
www.ADStransitions.com

A graduate of Baylor University College of Dentistry, Dr. Terry D. Watson practiced general dentistry in the Dallas area for more than 24 years. He founded Watson & Associates, Inc. dental brokerage firm in 1992. Dr. Watson remains an active member of the American Dental Association, Texas Dental Association and Dallas County Dental Society, and has served on numerous boards, including the ADA Financial Services, TDA Board of Directors and TDA Financial Services. He is a past president of the Dallas County Dental Society. In addition to his consulting work, Dr. Watson is a frequent lecturer at dental conferences and national seminars, speaking on practice transition and retirement planning, and has published articles on the topic in TDA Journal, *Dental Economics Magazine* and Dallas Academy of General Dentistry.

Watson, Brown & Associates provides practice appraisals, pre-planning for contingencies, partnership arrangements, brokerage and sales, associate arrangements, and start-up services with a common sense, bottom-line approach for dentists in Texas.